THE
CHEYENNE

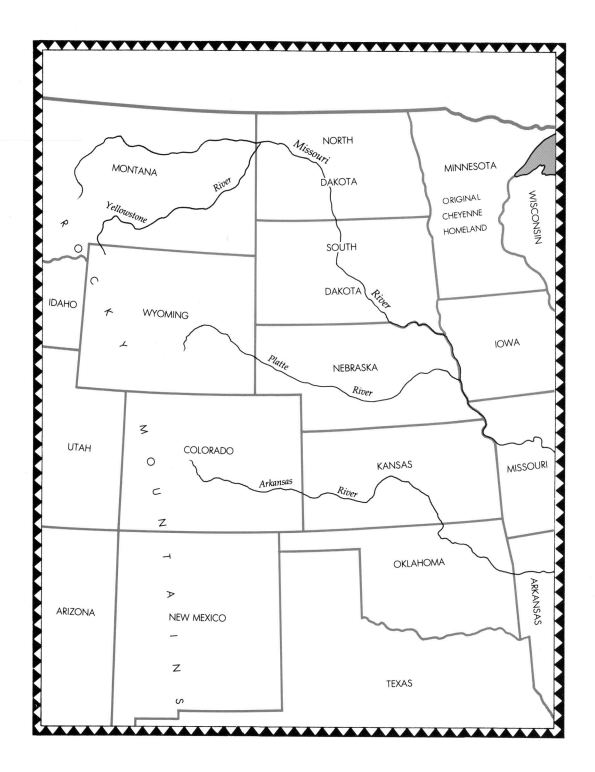

INDIANS OF NORTH AMERICA

THE
CHEYENNE

Stan Hoig
Central State University, Edmond, Oklahoma

Frank W. Porter III
General Editor

CHELSEA HOUSE PUBLISHERS
New York   Philadelphia

On the cover A painted Cheyenne shield (1870) made of leather, rawhide, cloth, and feathers.

Chelsea House Publishers
Editor-in-Chief Nancy Toff
Executive Editor Remmel T. Nunn
Managing Editor Karyn Gullen Browne
Copy Chief Juliann Barbato
Picture Editor Adrian G. Allen
Art Director Maria Epes
Manufacturing Manager Gerald Levine

Indians of North America
Senior Editor Sam Tanenhaus

Staff for **THE CHEYENNE**
Deputy Copy Chief Ellen Scordato
Editorial Assistant Clark Morgan
Assistant Art Director Laurie Jewell
Picture Researcher Elie Porter
Production Coordinator Joseph Romano

15 14 13 12 11 10

Library of Congress Cataloging in Publication Data

Hoig, Stan.
The Cheyenne / Stan Hoig : Frank W. Porter, III, general editor.
p. cm.—(Indians of North America)
Bibliography: p.
Includes index.
ISBN 1-55546-696-6
     0-7910-0358-2 (pbk.)
1. Cheyenne Indians. I. Porter, Frank W.,
1947– . II. Title. III. Series: Indians of North America (Chelsea House Publishers)
E99.C53H62 1989   88-17701
973'.0497—dc19   CIP

CONTENTS

INDIANS OF NORTH AMERICA

CHELSEA HOUSE PUBLISHERS

INDIANS OF NORTH AMERICA: CONFLICT AND SURVIVAL

Frank W. Porter III

The Indians survived our open intention of wiping them out, and since the tide turned they have even weathered our good intentions toward them, which can be much more deadly.

John Steinbeck
America and Americans

When Europeans first reached the North American continent, they found hundreds of tribes occupying a vast and rich country. The newcomers quickly recognized the wealth of natural resources. They were not, however, so quick or willing to recognize the spiritual, cultural, and intellectual riches of the people they called Indians.

The Indians of North America examines the problems that develop when people with different cultures come together. For American Indians, the consequences of their interaction with non-Indian people have been both productive and tragic. The Europeans believed they had "discovered" a "New World," but their religious bigotry, cultural bias, and materialistic world view kept them from appreciating and understanding the people who lived in it. All too often they attempted to change the way of life of the indigenous people. The Spanish conquistadores wanted the Indians as a source of labor. The Christian missionaries, many of whom were English, viewed them as potential converts. French traders and trappers used the Indians as a means to obtain pelts. As Francis Parkman, the 19th-century historian, stated, "Spanish civilization crushed the Indian; English civilization scorned and neglected him; French civilization embraced and cherished him."

Nearly 500 years later, many people think of American Indians as curious vestiges of a distant past, waging a futile war to survive in a Space Age society. Even today, our understanding of the history and culture of American Indians is too often derived from unsympathetic, culturally biased, and inaccurate reports. The American Indian, described and portrayed in thousands of movies, television programs, books, articles, and government studies, has either been raised to the status of the "noble savage" or disparaged as the "wild Indian" who resisted the westward expansion of the American frontier.

Where in this popular view are the real Indians, the human beings and communities whose ancestors can be traced back to ice-age hunters? Where are the creative and indomitable people whose sophisticated technologies used the natural resources to ensure their survival, whose military skill might even have prevented European settlement of North America if not for devastating epidemics and the disruption of the ecology? Where are the men and women who are today diligently struggling to assert their legal rights and express once again the value of their heritage?

The various Indian tribes of North America, like people everywhere, have a history that includes population expansion, adaptation to a range of regional environments, trade across wide networks, internal strife, and warfare. This was the reality. Europeans justified their conquests, however, by creating a mythical image of the New World and its native people. In this myth, the New World was a virgin land, waiting for the Europeans. The arrival of Christopher Columbus ended a timeless primitiveness for the original inhabitants.

Also part of this myth was the debate over the origins of the American Indians. Fantastic and diverse answers were proposed by the early explorers, missionaries, and settlers. Some thought that the Indians were descended from the Ten Lost Tribes of Israel, others that they were descended from inhabitants of the lost continent of Atlantis. One writer suggested that the Indians had reached North America in another Noah's ark.

A later myth, perpetrated by many historians, focused on the relentless persecution during the past five centuries until only a scattering of these "primitive" people remained to be herded onto reservations. This view fails to chronicle the overt and covert ways in which the Indians successfully coped with the intruders.

All of these myths presented one-sided interpretations that ignored the complexity of European and American events and policies. All left serious questions unanswered. What were the origins of the American Indians? Where did they come from? How and when did they get to the New World? What was their life—their culture—really like?

In the late 1800s, anthropologists and archaeologists in the Smithsonian Institution's newly created Bureau of American Ethnology in Washington, D. C., began to study scientifically the history and culture of the Indians of North America. They were motivated by an honest belief that the Indians were on the verge of extinction and that along with them would vanish their languages, religious beliefs, technology, myths, and legends. These men and women went out to visit, study, and record data from as many Indian communities as possible before this information was forever lost.

By this time there was a new myth in the national consciousness. American Indians existed as figures in the American past. They had performed a historical mission. They had challenged white settlers who trekked across the continent. Once conquered, however, they were supposed to accept graciously the way of life of their conquerors.

The reality again was different. American Indians resisted both actively and passively. They refused to lose their unique identity, to be assimilated into white society. Many whites viewed the Indians not only as members of a conquered nation but also as "inferior" and "unequal." The rights of the Indians could be expanded, contracted, or modified as the conquerors saw fit. In every generation, white society asked itself what to do with the American Indians. Their answers have resulted in the twists and turns of federal Indian policy.

There were two general approaches. One way was to raise the Indians to a "higher level" by "civilizing" them. Zealous missionaries considered it their Christian duty to elevate the Indian through conversion and scanty education. The other approach was to ignore the Indians until they disappeared under pressure from the ever-expanding white society. The myth of the "vanishing Indian" gave stronger support to the latter option, helping to justify the taking of the Indians' land.

Prior to the end of the 18th century, there was no national policy on Indians simply because the American nation had not yet come into existence. American Indians similarly did not possess a political or social unity with which to confront the various Europeans. They were not homogeneous. Rather, they were loosely formed bands and tribes, speaking nearly 300 languages and thousands of dialects. The collective identity felt by Indians today is a result of their common experiences of defeat and/or mistreatment at the hands of whites.

During the colonial period, the British crown did not have a coordinated policy toward the Indians of North America. Specific tribes (most notably the Iroquois and the Cherokee) became military and political pawns used by both the crown and the individual colonies. The success of the American Revolution brought no immediate change. When the United States acquired new territory from France and Mexico in the early 19th century, the federal government wanted to open this land to settlement by homesteaders. But the Indian tribes that lived on this land had signed treaties with European governments assuring their title to the land. Now the United States assumed legal responsibility for honoring these treaties.

At first, President Thomas Jefferson believed that the Louisiana Purchase contained sufficient land for both the Indians and the white population.

Within a generation, though, it became clear that the Indians would not be allowed to remain. In the 1830s the federal government began to coerce the eastern tribes to sign treaties agreeing to relinquish their ancestral land and move west of the Mississippi River. Whenever these negotiations failed, President Andrew Jackson used the military to remove the Indians. The southeastern tribes, promised food and transportation during their removal to the West, were instead forced to walk the "Trail of Tears." More than 4,000 men, women, and children died during this forced march. The "removal policy" was successful in opening the land to homesteaders, but it created enormous hardships for the Indians.

By 1871 most of the tribes in the United States had signed treaties ceding most or all of their ancestral land in exchange for reservations and welfare. The treaty terms were intended to bind both parties for all time. But in the General Allotment Act of 1887, the federal government changed its policy again. Now the goal was to make tribal members into individual landowners and farmers, encouraging their absorption into white society. This policy was advantageous to whites who were eager to acquire Indian land, but it proved disastrous for the Indians. One hundred thirty-eight million acres of reservation land were subdivided into tracts of 160, 80, or as little as 40 acres, and allotted to tribe members on an individual basis. Land owned in this way was said to have "trust status" and could not be sold. But the surplus land—all Indian land not allotted to individuals— was opened (for sale) to white settlers. Ultimately, more than 90 million acres of land were taken from the Indians by legal and illegal means.

The resulting loss of land was a catastrophe for the Indians. It was necessary to make it illegal for Indians to sell their land to non-Indians. The Indian Reorganization Act of 1934 officially ended the allotment period. Tribes that voted to accept the provisions of this act were reorganized, and an effort was made to purchase land within preexisting reservations to restore an adequate land base.

Ten years later, in 1944, federal Indian policy again shifted. Now the federal government wanted to get out of the "Indian business." In 1953 an act of Congress named specific tribes whose trust status was to be ended "at the earliest possible time." This new law enabled the United States to end unilaterally, whether the Indians wished it or not, the special status that protected the land in Indian tribal reservations. In the 1950s federal Indian policy was to transfer federal responsibility and jurisdiction to state governments, encourage the physical relocation of Indian peoples from reservations to urban areas, and hasten the termination, or extinction, of tribes.

Between 1954 and 1962 Congress passed specific laws authorizing the termination of more than 100 tribal groups. The stated purpose of the termination policy was to ensure the full and complete integration of Indians into American society. However, there is a less benign way to interpret this legislation. Even as termination was being discussed in Congress, 133 separate bills were introduced to permit the transfer of trust land ownership from Indians to non-Indians.

With the Johnson administration in the 1960s the federal government began to reject termination. In the 1970s yet another Indian policy emerged. Known as "self-determination," it favored keeping the protective role of the federal government while increasing tribal participation in, and control of, important areas of local government. In 1983 President Reagan, in a policy statement on Indian affairs, restated the unique "government to government" relationship of the United States with the Indians. However, federal programs since then have moved toward transferring Indian affairs to individual states, which have long desired to gain control of Indian land and resources.

As long as American Indians retain power, land, and resources that are coveted by the states and the federal government, there will continue to be a "clash of cultures," and the issues will be contested in the courts, Congress, the White House, and even in the international human rights community. To give all Americans a greater comprehension of the issues and conflicts involving American Indians today is a major goal of this series. These issues are not easily understood, nor can these conflicts be readily resolved. The study of North American Indian history and culture is a necessary and important step toward that comprehension. All Americans must learn the history of the relations between the Indians and the federal government, recognize the unique legal status of the Indians, and understand the heritage and cultures of the Indians of North America.

Even after guns entered Plains Indian culture, hunters pursued their prime game, buffalo, with bows and lances.

AN EARLY GLIMPSE

In 1806 a small band of mounted Cheyenne warriors arrived at the great bend of the Missouri River in what is now North Dakota. They had come to visit the Mandan and the Hidatsa (called *Gros Ventres*, or Big Bellies by French Traders), members of the Missouri River Indian federation who lived in villages composed of rounded mud huts. The Cheyenne, long at war with these two bands, now wanted to establish a peaceful trading relationship with them. As a gesture of goodwill, the Cheyenne invited the Mandan and the Hidatsa to send a delegation to the Cheyenne encampment near the Black Hills of South Dakota, where they could exchange corn, squash, and other produce for splendid Cheyenne horses. The Cheyenne offered to return to the Hidatsa a young boy they had captured in battle and held hostage for several years.

Some of the Mandan and the Hidatsa suspected treachery. In the past the Cheyenne had been aggressive and combative, and there was no reason to believe they had suddenly changed their ways. After some debate, however, the two bands accepted the Cheyenne offer and agreed to send a trading caravan to the Cheyenne encampment. Village leaders asked a visitor, Charles Mackenzie, a trader from Canada, to join the expedition and promised him two horse loads of furs as payment. Mackenzie agreed. Alexander Henry, another Canadian trader, also went along.

Fortunately, both men wrote excellent accounts of the meeting between these Indian tribes. They described, among other things, the imposing caravan that set out for the Cheyenne camp. It was led by a mounted Hidatsa chief. He held a long staff that flew an American flag as a sign of peace. It had been presented to the band in 1804 by American explorers Meriwether Lewis and William Clark during their historic trek to the Pacific Ocean.

The Hidatsa chief was flanked by two mounted war leaders. Next, in tight formation, came foot soldiers, 8 squads of 30 to 40 young warriors. Each wore gaudy paint and feathers, and they

During their 1804 expedition, which passed through the Great Plains, Lewis and Clark met with many American Indian tribes. The calumet—or peace pipe—played an important role in negotiations.

were equipped with bows, arrows, lances, battle-axes, and shields. As they marched, these warriors shook rattles made of red deer hooves and at intervals sang and shouted. Behind them followed a group of older men, and in the rear walked women and children bearing provisions. All told, the expedition included more than 900 people.

For five days they traveled south, crossing three rivers—the Clearwater, the Heart, and the Cannonball—into Cheyenne territory. In the report Mackenzie filed with the North-West Trading Company, he described the abundant wildlife he saw:

Immense herds of buffaloes quench[ed] their thirst at these rivers and repos[ed] on their banks. . . . There were numerous flocks of red and fallow deer, the most of which, in the height of the day, were lying on the sides of the hills, while others were on the watch sniffing the fresh breeze while their companions indulged in a watchful slumber. There were also several muddy creeks, with a little water here and there, which the beavers had conserved by stopping the course of the outlets.

On the morning of the sixth day the trading caravan came upon the Cheyenne. They saw first a solid wall of horsemen, more than 100 strong. Each horseman brandished brightly feathered shields and lances draped with scalp locks. The warriors' high-spirited horses came from huge herds tended by the Cheyenne on meadows near their camp. The visitors noted the animals' size and strength and their frightening masks, which resembled the heads of wild beasts. Red cloth trimmed their mouths and nostrils, giving them a demonic appearance. Behind this formidable wall of horses and riders stood the Cheyenne foot soldiers.

It was a tense moment as the old enemies, both assembled in large numbers, silently faced one another. All eyes turned toward a handsome black stallion mounted by an imposing war leader clad in a blue coat and a striped blanket of Spanish make. The warrior suddenly pressed his horse into a gallop and sped toward the American flag held forward by the Hidatsa. The Cheyenne warrior accepted the proffered banner and embraced the chief. All the other Cheyenne then rode forward to greet their visitors and lead them toward their camp.

Outside the Cheyenne camp lay stacks of long, barkless poles used to make travois—vehicles that could be loaded with goods and dragged by dogs or horses. The hub of the camp consisted of a horseshoe-shaped arrangement of some 120 tipis—cone-shaped lodges made of buffalo hides. Their cross-poles, poking through a circle at the top, glistened in the morning sun. Long strips of buffalo meat hung drying on racks. Black-haired Cheyenne women busied themselves with various tasks. Some stretched and pegged hides onto the ground; others dressed buffalo robes or worked the pelts of smaller game with straw and porcupine quills.

Upon entering the camp, the visitors received a warm welcome—at first. Then more newcomers arrived, a small band of Assiniboin (a Canadian border tribe) that had trailed the expedition. The Hidatsa and Mandan greeted these surprise guests hospitably, but their hosts were furious. The Cheyenne held a long-standing grudge against the Assiniboin, who in years past had destroyed Cheyenne villages. The Cheyenne wanted to kill the newcomers, but their visitors resisted. The goodwill of the Cheyenne dissolved into sullen anger. They remained hostile throughout the meeting.

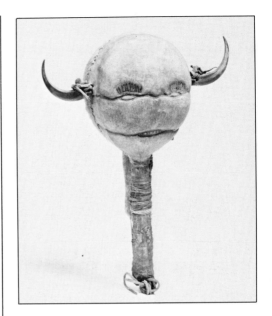

Cheyenne war preparations included shaking war rattles such as this rawhide piece. It has horns made of eagle claws and is adorned with a lock of horsehair.

Even the promised return of the Gros Ventres boy went off badly. The procedure for recovering the captive involved a ceremony that featured the calumet, a long-stemmed pipe with a red clay head and ornaments of feather and scalp locks. The calumet was placed on a length of red cloth by a Gros Ventres priest, while other tribe members danced and sang to the beating of drums and shaking of rattles. After this a buffalo skull, its eyes and nostrils stuffed with hay, was placed on an offering shroud—an altar heaped with guns and ammunition presented as gifts. Custom called for the Cheyenne to respond by offering horses. But they held back their fine mounts and instead brought forth only lame and scabby nags. At last, they presented the captive boy, wrapped in the American flag, but the ritual abruptly concluded without further ceremony. Fearful that blood might be spilled, the Gros Ventres and Mandan made a cautious retreat from the Cheyenne camp.

The account of this episode by Mackenzie and Henry was the first by whites to provide an in-depth view of the Cheyenne at the height of their power, when the tribe roamed freely on the Great Plains. Before then—in fact, as late as the 17th century—the Cheyenne lived west of the Great Lakes, probably in what is now northern Minnesota. In the late 17th century, the tribe migrated farther west and settled on the Red River of the North where it divides Minnesota from North Dakota. Soon they established contacts with the

Mandan, Gros Ventres, and other tribes. Like them, the Cheyenne built villages made of earthen dwellings and became farmers, growing corn, beans, and squash.

Cheyenne culture changed dramatically in the late 18th century when other tribes introduced them to horses, which had been brought to the New World by Spanish explorers. By 1830 the tribe had become master horse breeders and riders. They forsook farming for hunting and abandoned permanent village life for the nomadic existence appropriate to the pursuit of the large herds of bison, or buffalo, that roamed the grassy prairies of the Great Plains. As a result, the Cheyenne became a major presence in a vast area of the American West, ranging as far south as New Mexico and as far north as Montana.

The survival of the Cheyenne depended on huge herds of buffalo that roamed the Plains in the 19th century.

By 1868, when this engraving appeared in Harper's Weekly, *the Cheyenne were at war with intruders such as these fur traders, who propel their keelboat along the Missouri River while warriors fire at them from a bluff.*

In these same years—the mid-19th century—the United States began to expand its borders westward. Traders, immigrants, and the U.S. Army steadily streamed into the open wilds the Cheyenne considered their own. The tribe tried to drive off these intruders, but they were too numerous, and the Cheyenne became resigned to sharing their land with the U.S. government. Sadly, even this arrangement failed, as the huge buffalo herds—the tribe's staple game—were slaughtered wholesale by white hunters. Inevitably, the differences between two opposing cultures led to armed conflict. From 1857 to 1879, the Cheyenne fought an ongoing war with the U.S. Army. The tribe scored some victories, including the celebrated battle at Little Bighorn, where they helped the Sioux fight General George Armstrong Custer and his troops in 1876.

In the end, though, the Cheyenne had no chance of defeating so powerful a foe, and in the 1880s they surrendered and accepted removal to reservations. Some Cheyenne ended up in the Indian Territory of Oklahoma. Others went to Montana. They remain there to this day, where they struggle to keep alive their own rich heritage despite the demands of the larger society that rules them. That struggle echoes with the remembrance of a long and glorious history. ▲

High-Backed Wolf was the ideal Cheyenne chief—compassionate, wise, and strong. He sat for this portrait by George Catlin in 1832.

2

MEN AND WOMEN, WAR AND PEACE

The first contact between whites and the Cheyenne occurred in 1680 when a group of Indians visited the French explorer Sieur de La Salle while he was building Ft. Crevecoeur on the Illinois River. These people spoke the tongue of the Algonkian, who populated a vast region north of the Great Lakes and called themselves *Tsis-tsis'-tas*, or "the People."

At this time the tribe was known as the Chaa. They resided on the banks of the Minnesota River in earth-covered lodges. A peaceful people, they made pottery and ate small deer, rabbits, fish, bird eggs, berries, and roots. The Chaa remained in this area until the early 18th century, when a larger nation, the Sioux, pushed them west into North Dakota. There they settled along another river, the Sheyenne, and built earth-lodge villages. They became planters, raising corn, beans, and squash.

Throughout these years, the Cheyenne were a sedentary, peaceful people. They suffered attacks from larger tribes, such as the Cree, Ojibway, Sioux, and the Assiniboin, who overran and badly mauled them in about 1740. The few survivors fled southwest across the Missouri River and near the Black Hills of South Dakota. One band was massacred by a large party of Sioux.

Also at this time, the Cheyenne acquired horses, which had been brought north from the Great Plains by the Comanche, Kiowa, and other tribes. Horses changed the culture of the Cheyenne in two crucial ways. First, Cheyenne men, often tall and lithe, adapted so effectively to mounted battle that they quickly became among the most feared of all Indian warriors. They now were a match for larger tribes that had formerly defeated them. Second, the Cheyenne became highly skilled hunters. Previously, they had been handicapped at bagging buffalo, mainly because the lack of horses required the entire band to form a "surround," driving the animals into a small area where

19

The Sioux introduced the Cheyenne to tipis, dwellings made from 11 to 21 tanned buffalo hides. These portable lodges ideally suited the nomadic culture of buffalo hunters.

they could be trapped and killed. Horses enabled individual Cheyenne hunters to slay the animals by the chase.

The Cheyenne began to hunt the game that roamed in huge herds across the Great Plains, especially the buffalo, which proved invaluable to the Cheyenne. Their meat and the chunky tallow fat provided food in both winter and summer. Buffalo hide could be tanned into leather for ropes, horse gear, and other essential goods. Buffalo skin also furnished the coverings for a new kind of abode, tipis (introduced to the Cheyenne by the Sioux). These dwellings featured a central fire, and along the

sides were beds made of thick, matted robes (also taken from the buffalo) that provided warmth against the bitter cold of winter. Because tipis were portable, they enabled Cheyenne warriors to take their families with them rather than leave them behind in unprotected villages when they ventured onto the plains.

The Cheyenne prospered on the plains. Their population grew, and they gained strength through alliances with the Arapaho and the Sioux. By the end of the 18th century, the Cheyenne had begun warring with other tribes of the northern plains. No written accounts of their early conquests exist, but Mandan robes decorated with symbolic artwork often include depictions of battles with Cheyenne warriors.

The Mandan were not their only foes. Cheyenne war parties riding westward came into conflict with the Crow, who lived in the Bighorn River country of Wyoming and Montana; the Shoshone, who lived along the Sweetwater River in Wyoming; and the Ute, who inhabited the eastern slopes of the Rocky Mountains in Colorado. In addition, the Cheyenne helped defeat the Kiowa and drive them south from their home along the Platte River of Wyoming and Nebraska.

"These lands once belonged to the Kiowas and the Crows," Black Hawk, an Oglala Sioux chief, once boasted to United States peace commissioners, "but we whipped these nations out of them. We met the Kiowas and whipped them, at the Kiowa Creek, just below where we now are. We met them and whipped them again and the last time at Crow Creek. This last battle was fought by the Cheyennes, Arapahoes and Ogallahlah [Oglala] combined." The Cheyenne's most persistent enemy was the Pawnee, who lived along the Loup River in Nebraska. The prize in this contest was an extensive buffalo range that covered western Kansas and Nebraska. In their effort to protect their claim to this area, the Pawnee often allied with eastern tribes such as the Sac, Fox, and Delaware. The Cheyenne, for their part, teamed up with their Arapaho confederates. Buffalo were not the only goal. The Cheyenne also invaded the ranges south of the Arkansas River to raid the enormous horse herds owned by the Comanche and other tribes.

In the 19th century, Cheyenne culture featured three dangerous activities, each a test of bravery and skill: hunting, horse stealing, and fighting. At an early age, males learned that status within the tribe was linked to the ability to handle weapons and stalk prey. Cheyenne men hunted all sorts of game, including large animals such as antelope, deer, elk, wild sheep, and, of course, buffalo. And they tracked down smaller beasts, especially wolves and foxes for their fur. Buffalo remained their staple, however, and the Cheyenne refined techniques for hunting them. The hunter spent long hours training his horse to ride close to the animal, so that both his hands would be free to use his bow and arrow. A

A Cheyenne warrior photographed in 1875. Most Cheyenne warriors belonged to one of five tribal military societies.

These Cheyenne were photographed at their summer encampment in 1895. Meat dries on the poles outside the tipi.

powerful hunter could shoot an arrow so forcefully that it passed cleanly through one buffalo and penetrated the hide of another. Spears also made good weapons for killing buffalo.

Also valuable to the Cheyenne were horses. Without them one could not cover the vast stretches of the prairie. A good war pony was easily a man's most precious possession. The Cheyenne procured the animals any way they could. Warriors raided the fleet herds that raced across the southern ranges. An even greater feat was stealing horses from other tribes. Plains Indians viewed this thievery not as a crime, but as a noble deed requiring courage and skill.

The Cheyenne vied with other tribes that hunted the buffalo on the Great Plains. Warriors developed ways of measuring their prowess, in order to win respect within the tribe. One test was the counting of coups, wherein the warrior touched his enemy with a long, crook-ended stick. Like scalp taking, this form of conquest enabled a young warrior to make his mark within the tribe. Coups earned him the admiration of the entire band. When warriors returned to the domestic world of the camp, everyone—including eligible young women—turned out to celebrate their war exploits.

The Cheyenne also paid tribute to war skills through five military societies—Fox, Elk, Shield, Dog, and Bowstring. Each club had its own distinctive style of dress and its own dances and songs. In organization, however, all the clubs were similar. Each, for instance, had four leaders: Two acted as war chiefs and decision makers; two served as messengers and ambassadors to the other clubs and to the tribe's peace leaders. One military society, the Dog Soldiers, became the most notorious and most feared warriors on the Great Plains in the 19th century, when the Cheyenne battled the expanding republic of the United States. The Dog Soldiers came to constitute a band of their own, the only one whose membership was restricted to certain clans, a group of Indians tracing their descent to a common ancestor.

Although the Cheyenne were accomplished warriors, the most esteemed members of their tribe were their chiefs, who were responsible for peace within the tribe and with outside nations. A Cheyenne chief usually had distinguished himself as a warrior but prided himself on his ability to maintain harmony for his people. Each chief was chosen for a 10-year term that could not be revoked for any reason.

Chiefs had to be exemplary men— calm, generous, kind, sympathetic, courageous, and self-sacrificing. They routinely lavished gifts on the poor and unfortunate, even on enemies. In *The Cheyenne Way*, a study published in 1941, researchers K. N. Llewellyn and E. A. Hoebel cite the example of High-backed Wolf, a chief who once came upon a Pawnee beaten and left naked by Cheyenne warriors. "I am going to

help you out," the chief announced to the stricken man. "Here are your clothes. Outside are three horses. You may take your choice! Here is a mountain lion skin."

As anthropologist G. B. Grinnell wrote in his classic 1923 work, *The Cheyenne Indians: Their History and Way of Life*: "A good chief gave his whole heart and his whole mind to the work of helping his people, and strove for their welfare with an earnestness and a devotion rarely equaled by the rulers of other men. . . . True friends, delightful companions, wise counselors, they were men whose attitude toward their fellows we might all emulate." Their compassion sometimes exceeded the bounds of reason. A chief would not protest when another man ran off with his wife; he might even refuse the compensation offered by the culprit—a pipe, horse, and other gifts—because to accept them was to admit being wounded by the loss, which would dent the chief's dignity.

At any time, 44 chiefs— 4 from each of their 10 bands plus the 4 principal chiefs—formed the council that governed the entire Cheyenne nation. Within this council four chiefs attained a special status that combined governmental and religious functions. First came the head priest-chief, called the Sweet Medicine Chief. He was entrusted with a sacred package of grass—the Sweet Medicine Bundle— that he inherited from his predecessor and passed on to his successor. During meetings in the council tipi, or lodge, he occupied a special seat called *heum* (meaning "the above"). It signified that he was the mortal representative of the deity who ruled the earth, itself symbolized by the circle scooped out of the ground at the foot of his ceremonial seat.

This circle was surrounded by sticks. One corresponded to Sweet Medicine Chief, and the other sticks corresponded to the other leading chiefs. These men represented divine spirits such as the Big Holy People, or Those Who Know Everything; Where the Food Comes From; and the Spirit Who Gives Good Health. Thus, these chiefs were emissaries of the benevolent forces that ruled Cheyenne life.

At council meetings, the chiefs decided various issues, such as whether to move camp or to form alliances with other tribes. The council also resolved judicial matters. They decreed what punishment should be meted out to lawbreakers and resolved feuds that threatened the harmony of the tribe. Each meeting began with several minutes of silence. Then one of the oldest, most experienced men introduced an issue for debate. No one ever interrupted another speaker, and all men freely voiced their views. In summer the sides of the tipi were rolled up, and a large audience might gather to hear the deliberations. Once a decision was reached, the chiefs informed their bands and explained what action would be taken and why.

Hunting, thieving, warring, and lawmaking fell to men, but much that was essential to Cheyenne culture was

A Cheyenne scrapes hide, one of the many steps necessary for making buckskin.

the province of women, who ruled the all-important domestic sphere. One major chore was gathering the food for the family. This was often no easy task. A favorite vegetable, turnips, had to be dug out of the ground, boiled, sliced, and then dried in the sun. Thornier yet was the process of collecting the fruit that sprouted on the prickly pear cactus. First, women yanked clumps of fruit off the plant and stuck them in a *parfleche* (rawhide bag). Next they brushed away the spines with brooms made of twigs. Then, their fingers protected by deerskin thimbles, they carefully picked the fruit clean. Finally, they separated the seeds and dried the rest in the sun. The result was a tasty thickener for stews and soups.

Women spent most of their time fixing meals, tanning hides, and sewing clothing. When the band moved camp, women rolled up the hide walls of the tipi and—when the band resettled—rolled them back down. If it seemed the site would be permanent, women modeled their tipis into comfortable homes, with raised mats, grass-covered "benches" (made of sod), and cupboards ingeniously formed of buffalo robes. The work women did on their dwellings was prized by the entire band, and no man could cross the threshold of a new tipi until a brave warrior first stepped into it and was followed by other esteemed men.

The many chores performed by Cheyenne women required a variety of tools that they devised themselves. One was a stone maul, or hammer, with a willow-branch handle. It was used to pound tipi pegs into the ground, chop firewood, and shatter animal bones for soup. Women also kept several spoons made of steamed or boiled horns removed from slain buffalo or sheep. Every Cheyenne woman owned a set of tools for tanning, the painstaking process whereby tough animal hide was softened into pliable material.

Once hide was tanned and dried, women sewed it into garments. For themselves they fashioned several skins into long dresses that hung below the knee. For men they made long-sleeved shirts, fringed leggings, and breechcloths—square skins tied around the waist with a cord. Men and women alike wore moccasins, which had rawhide soles and were beautifully embellished with beads. The most elaborate clothing of all was the decorated, or quilled, robe. To make one, a woman needed the sponsorship of the Quillers' Society, an exclusive club, like the military societies. Its members instructed

Cheyenne used implements such as this flesher, made from buffalo bone, to scrape hides clean.

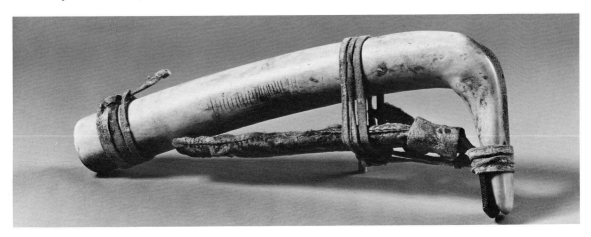

others and obeyed hallowed rituals, such as delivering recitations in which they named the best garments they had ever sewn.

One of the most remarkable qualities exhibited by Cheyenne women was their chastity. Traders and travelers often praised their modesty and diffidence, and Cheyenne men honored them for it. A suitor might wait five years before his beloved would agree to marry him. And he would not dream of embarrassing her by posing the question directly. Instead, he enlisted an aged relative—often a woman—who approached the girl's family with gifts. After stating the young man's case, she promptly left the family alone to discuss the matter privately. The next day, they announced their decision.

If the marriage was approved, the bride was clad in her loveliest buckskin dress, placed upon the finest horse owned by her family, and led by an old woman—never a relative—to the house of the groom. His relatives lifted the bride off the horse, set her on a ceremonial blanket, and then carried her across the threshold. The groom's female relatives clothed her in new finery, dressed her hair, and painted her face. The ceremony concluded with a feast. Afterward, the bride's mother supplied the couple with a new tipi and furnishings, and both families contributed household items. The newlyweds took up residence near the bride's home. Prosperous men might take several wives, each of whom belonged to his extended family, and each inhabit-

Cheyenne men gather outside the Sun Dance lodge, the site of the Renewal of the Medicine Arrows—a ceremony that drew the entire tribe together.

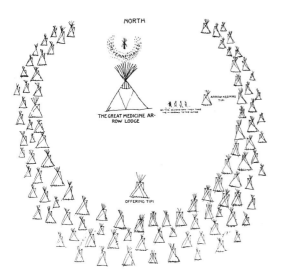

This drawing shows the layout of a camp during the Medicine Arrow rite. The family tipis formed a crescent, with lodges placed inside it.

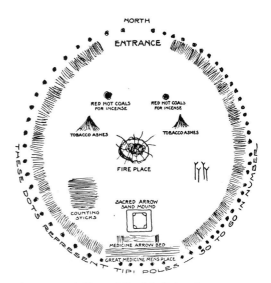

A representation of the Medicine Arrow lodge interior shows the placement of objects used in the rite.

ing her own tipi with her children.

The marriage ceremony was only one of many observed by the Cheyenne. Their culture included a larger body of social lore, some of it adopted from other tribes, some of it originated by themselves. One hallowed ritual unique to the Cheyenne was the Renewal of the Medicine (or Sacred) Arrows. It developed after the tribe underwent the great societal change created when they became hunters and warriors. The ceremony fell on the longest day of the year. On this day, the entire tribe—all 10 bands—moved to an open area watered by a stream and placed their tipis in a wide circle.

Within the circle stood the lodge of the Keeper of the Arrows, and in the exact center stood a huge tipi, the Sa-

cred Arrow Lodge. Inside it, priests opened a bundle that held the arrows. Cheyenne belief held that two of these arrows, when aimed at the buffalo, reduced the beasts to powerlessness, and that the other two arrows had the same effect on human enemies. After the conclusion of the Renewal Ceremony, all the participants purified themselves in a lodge before they could resume their role in ordinary life.

Cheyenne rituals also included several dances. One, the Sun Dance, was practiced by a number of Plains Indian tribes. It lasted eight days and was highlighted by a grisly dance performed by young men whose chests were implanted with leather thongs tethered to a lodge pole. These torturous conditions tested the warriors' tolerance of

THE SUN DANCE CEREMONY

Cheyenne and other Plains Indian tribes performed the Sun Dance in order to revitalize and replenish the natural world with earth, water, wind, and herds of buffalo.

According to tribal tradition, the Sun Dance originated during a time of famine among the Cheyenne. In order to alleviate the suffering of his people, a Cheyenne named Erect Horns and his wife made a pilgrimage to the Sacred Mountain to seek guidance from the Great Spirit. The Great Spirit told Erect Horns that he must sponsor a Sun Dance, and he instructed him in the intricacies of the ceremony. Ever since, Sun Dances have become a regular part of Cheyenne ritual.

The ceremony begins when a male member of the tribe—sometimes called "The Multiplier" or "The Reproducer" because the tribe is reborn through his act of generosity—announces that he is organizing the ceremony. The sponsor then retreats with his wife and the tribal priests into the Lone Tipi, raised as a symbol of the Sacred Mountain.

For four days those isolated inside the Lone Tipi symbolically reenact Erect Horns's visit to the Great Spirit. They also perform sacred rites of regeneration, such as shaping the tipi's dirt floor into five mounds (each symbolizing the earth). On the fourth day, the priests consecrate a buffalo skull, thereby guaranteeing that the herds will abound for the rest of the year.

During the four days of Lone Tipi rites, the rest of the camp gathers to build a Sun Dance lodge, a central pole encircled by a ring of upright wooden posts, all joined at the top by long, horizontal strips of timber. The Cheyenne then cover this structure with the buffalo robes of celebrated warriors. When the priests emerge from the Lone Tipi, they bless the lodge and offer prayers to the Great Spirit.

The dance itself begins when warriors—their faces decorated with ceremonial paint—gather around the lodge's central pole and rise repeatedly up and down on their toes, blowing through eagle-bone whistles held between their teeth. They repeat this activity for four days, stopping only to eat and drink.

After the dancing ends, Cheyenne warriors conclude the Sun Dance with ritual torture. Several men pierce the faces, chests, or backs of their comrades with sharpened skewers. This painful ceremony is thought to arouse the pity of spirits. Yet it is also an important rite of passage for males, an occasion for them to display publicly their bravery and capacity to endure pain. After the eight-day ceremony concludes, the Cheyenne leave the Sun Dance lodge confident that they have revitalized the natural world around them.

Once the Medicine Arrow ceremony concluded, all the participants cleansed themselves in a sweat lodge, such as this one.

extreme physical pain. A second dance included men and women dressed as animals. They performed zany, or *mass-a'ne*, antics as they tried to elude hunters who belonged to the Bowstring Society.

Cheyenne religious beliefs influenced their relationship with whites, whom they regarded with superstition, possibly because of an incident that occurred in 1795. That year "the Lance," a Cheyenne chief, accepted gifts from a French trader and promised, in return, to treat strangers hospitably. The Lance broke his vow and murdered a Sioux and his family living among the Cheyenne. Soon after, three of the Lance's children died. Next, lightning struck the hut inhabited by his brother, who was killed along with his family and even his dogs and horses.

The Cheyenne developed the belief that white people were bad omens. A typical incident occurred in 1804, when the Lewis and Clark expedition met them at a Mandan village while en route to the Pacific Ocean. As a token of friendship, Captain Clark offered a Cheyenne chief the gift of a small medal. Instead of being pleased, the chief grew alarmed. He explained that, in his view, white people were "medicine" and therefore must be shown homage. He accepted the gift only after Clark consented to accept a robe and buffalo meat in exchange. Eventually, the Cheyenne would find more concrete reasons for distrusting whites. ▲

Trader George Bent married a Cheyenne woman, Magpie, the daughter of Chief Black Kettle. In this photograph, taken in 1867, she wears a dress made of elk skin and teeth. Bent lived for many years among the Cheyenne.

FRIENDS
AND
ENEMIES

In the early 1800s, the Cheyenne resided on the Cheyenne River near the Black Hills, although they had begun to winter in Colorado near the headwaters of two large rivers. One, the South Platte, ran east; the other, the Arkansas, emptied into the Gulf of Mexico. The Cheyenne headed south for several reasons: to spend the winter in a warmer climate, to raid the huge herds of wild horses kept by some southern tribes, and to hunt bear and beaver, which filled the southern edge of the Rocky Mountains in north central Colorado, near present-day Denver. Come spring, the Cheyenne returned north to trade their skins and horses to the Missouri River tribes or to white traders.

Soon the Cheyenne began a larger migration, one that relocated much of the tribe. The way was opened in the 18th century, when the large Comanche nation moved from the northern Rockies into the horse-rich lower plains and forced the Apache south. In the wake

of the Comanche came the Kiowa. These tribes ultimately became allied and formed a single entity. Their departure from the high plains east of the Rockies left a vacuum into which the Cheyenne moved. Initially, they ventured south on only a temporary basis: As late as 1825, the majority of the Cheyenne population still lived near the Black Hills. About this time, the tribe separated into two groups. Some Cheyenne bands preferred the northern country; others began to take up permanent residence along the Arkansas River in southern Colorado. There was no enmity between the two groups; they maintained their clan and family contacts. But they pulled apart: The Southern Cheyenne remained in their new home, and the Northern Cheyenne roamed west from the Black Hills to the high country of Wyoming and Montana along the North Platte, the Powder, and the Tongue rivers. As time passed, the split became more distinct.

In 1828 the Southern Cheyenne found a powerful incentive to remain in Colorado. That year, Missourians Charles and William Bent, trappers and traders, had a fateful encounter with a party of Cheyenne who had come south to catch wild horses. The Cheyenne party was led by Yellow Wolf, a highly intelligent chief. The Bents proposed opening regular trade relations with Yellow Wolf. The chief agreed and suggested that the white men locate down-river from the mountains and away from the buffalo range. If they would do so, he said, he would bring his band and others there to trade.

Accordingly, the Bents constructed a log-and-adobe mud fort at the point where the Arkansas and Purgatoire rivers converged in the flatlands of southeast Colorado. Later known as Ft. William or Bent's Fort, this permanent trading post became a stopping place for countless whites who traversed the plains along the Santa Fe Trail, the pioneer route that reached from Missouri to New Mexico. Many famous men of the West would be associated with Bent's Fort, including Kit Carson, who was a Bent trader for a time before becoming a Western explorer, guide, and Indian fighter. The Bents themselves went on to accomplish a great deal in the West. Charles Bent was appointed governor of the New Mexico Territory, and William married a Cheyenne woman, had children by her, and became deeply involved in frontier Indian affairs.

Before he became an explorer and Indian fighter, Kit Carson worked as a trader at Bent's Fort.

The construction of Bent's Fort signaled the beginning of a new phase of Cheyenne history, as whites began to encroach on the Great Plains. For the time being, however, the Cheyenne welcomed Bent's Fort and the steady traffic of immigrants who journeyed along the Arkansas River. Mexicans trekked up from Taos, New Mexico, and American and French traders arrived. These men regularly visited and sometimes lived among the Cheyenne, bringing them goods from the outside world.

Not long before the Bents set up their trading post, the Cheyenne formally met official representatives of the United States. This episode occurred in June 1820, when the U.S. government sent a group of 19 mounted Americans led by Stephen H. Long on an expedition up the Missouri and Platte rivers. Long explored as far west as the Rocky Mountains, contacting Indians living in the region. The party divided when it reached the Arkansas River. Long took nine of the men south to explore the headwaters of the Red River. Captain J. R. Bell led the others on a return trip along the Arkansas and met a party of Cheyenne near the mouth of the Purgatoire River.

In 1825, when the majority of the Cheyenne still lived near the Black Hills, they were visited by General Henry Atkinson and U.S. Indian agent Benjamin O'Fallon, who had been appointed by President James Monroe to sign treaties with the tribes they encountered. The emissaries were escorted by 476 troops sent along to impress the Indians with the power and importance of the United States.

The expedition proceeded up the Missouri River in flat-bottomed, or keel, boats fitted with manually operated paddlewheels and also with sails and oars. The party included mounted

In June 1820, Stephen H. Long led an expedition down the Missouri River. He met Cheyenne near the Rocky Mountains.

hunters who rode along the riverbank chasing game to feed the voyagers. On July 4, 1825, at the mouth of the Teton River, Atkinson signed a treaty with the great Cheyenne chief High-backed Wolf, another chief (named Little Moon), and others.

By signing the Treaty of 1825, the Cheyenne acknowledged the supremacy of the United States government, which, in turn, promised the tribe protection and friendship. The treaty spelled out trade agreements, included mutual guarantees of safe passage for Americans passing through Indian country, and prohibited the sale of arms

A Cheyenne woman and child, photographed in the late 19th century. In the first decades of the 1800s, enemy tribes often staged raids on the Cheyenne to steal their horses and take female tribe members and children captive.

by traders to tribes unfriendly to the United States.

Atkinson's party was impressed by the Cheyenne. These Indians seemed purer than white men—noble savages, unspoiled children of nature: "They have unlike other Indians all the virtues that nature can give without the vices of civilization," wrote an officer in a letter to the Washington, D.C. *Daily National Intelligencer*. "They are artless, fearless, and live in constant exercise of moral and Christian virtues, though they know it not."

Another member of Atkinson's party, a journalist, noted that High-backed Wolf was one of the most dignified and elegant-looking men he had ever seen. This opinion was echoed by painter George Catlin, who executed portraits of both the chief and his comely wife, She Who Bathes Her Knees. The painting shows High-backed Wolf dressed in an Indian deerskin suit handsomely adorned with porcupine quills. His wife wears a dress made of mountain sheepskin decorated with quills and beads. Less than a decade later, High-backed Wolf would die at the hands of his own people while trying to keep the peace in a tribal argument. The death of this great leader widened the rift between the Northern and Southern Cheyenne and encouraged the southern migration of many Cheyenne.

Even as the Cheyenne formed valuable friendships with white traders, they remained at odds with other Indians. In 1825 a party of Northern Cheyenne Bowstring warriors was massacred in a battle against the Crow on the Tongue River. The Cheyenne wanted vengeance and sent emissaries to the Sioux, who agreed to join them in raising an armed force. These warriors located a Crow camp and made a surprise attack at dawn. They overran the camp and seized many women and children as captives. Later, the Crows were permitted to visit Cheyenne villages and to recover the captives, though—as often happened—some of the Crow women had already become Cheyenne wives and mothers.

Another enemy was the Comanche, whose large horse herds the Cheyenne often raided. After one sortie, the Comanche chief Bull Hump led a war party that located the Cheyenne encampment in Colorado on the South Platte River. The Comanche raided their herds and headed south with a large number of horses—their own and some taken from the Cheyenne. They had reached the Arkansas River when Yellow Wolf discovered them and led his warriors in a dawn attack, stampeding the horses. A fight took place, and the Cheyenne, armed with guns—the Comanche had only bows and arrows—forced their foes to retreat, leaving behind their horses and a few warriors.

In the late 1830s, the Southern Cheyenne battled the Pawnee after they had wiped out an entire party of Cheyenne horse thieves. The Cheyenne did not retaliate immediately. Instead they waited out the winter. When spring arrived, they "moved the Medicine Arrows"—took up arms—against the Pawnee. A large contingent of Arapaho and Sioux joined the Cheyenne offensive.

During the ensuing battle, the Keeper of the Arrows tied the sacred weapons to the head of his lance and carried them into the fight. As the opposing sides squared off, a Pawnee suffering from an illness seated himself between the lines, evidently to await his death. The Keeper of the Arrows charged at him, but the Pawnee grabbed the lance and jerked away the arrows. Several Cheyenne made a fierce charge in an attempt to recover them, but some Pawnee got to their comrade first and made off with the Medicine Arrows. The Cheyenne killed the ailing Pawnee, but the loss of the sacred arrows dampened their spirits, and they gave up the fight. The incident was followed by intense mourning at various Cheyenne camps. Women and children wailed in despair, and warriors sheared off their hair. The Cheyenne never recovered the arrows, but they got revenge in 1833 when they surrounded a Pawnee war party on foot in the hills near Bent's Fort and slaughtered every last man. The site became known as the "Pawnee Hills."

The Cheyenne continued pilfering horses from the southern tribes, leading to still another clash between Yellow Wolf and Bull Hump in 1836. Following a Cheyenne raid on a Comanche herd on the north fork of the Red River, Bull Hump once again set out to recover his mounts. He and his men tracked the herd past Bent's Fort. Fortunately he did not spot the prize stallion that Yellow Wolf had presented to William Bent. The animal was named "Yellow Wolf," and ultimately became a hunting horse for Kit Carson.

Once again the Cheyenne succeeded in stealing Comanche horses. But their luck ran out the following year when a party of 48 Bowstring warriors went south on foot to filch mounts from the Kiowa herds. The entire group was discovered, killed, and scalped by the Kiowa and Comanche. Yellow Wolf and other Cheyenne leaders were determined to avenge this defeat. An opportunity arose in 1838 when a combined force of Cheyenne and Arapaho warriors located a Comanche-Kiowa encampment in Oklahoma. The Cheyenne-Arapaho party was discovered as it approached the Comanche-Kiowa camp and was met in force about a mile away. In a clash of charging warriors, the defenders were slowly beaten back and the village overrun. The Comanche and Kiowa women made a futile effort to survive by digging trenches in which they tried to hide with their children.

The resulting massacre halted only when the Cheyenne learned that a company of U.S. dragoons and Osage scouts was already on its way to pay the Comanche a visit. This news caused the Cheyenne to retreat. They left 14 fallen comrades along with 58 dead Comanche and Kiowa and more than 100 slain horses.

The Battle of Wolf Creek led to a large peace council in 1840. It was held at Bent's Fort and was attended by the Cheyenne, Arapaho, Comanche, Kiowa, and Prairie Apache. After festivities that included a feast, music, singing, dancing, and an exchange of gifts, the tribes agreed upon a friendship pact. This pact granted the Cheyenne and Arapaho the privilege to range freely south of the Arkansas River.

HISTORICAL TRACE OF THE CHEYENNE NATION

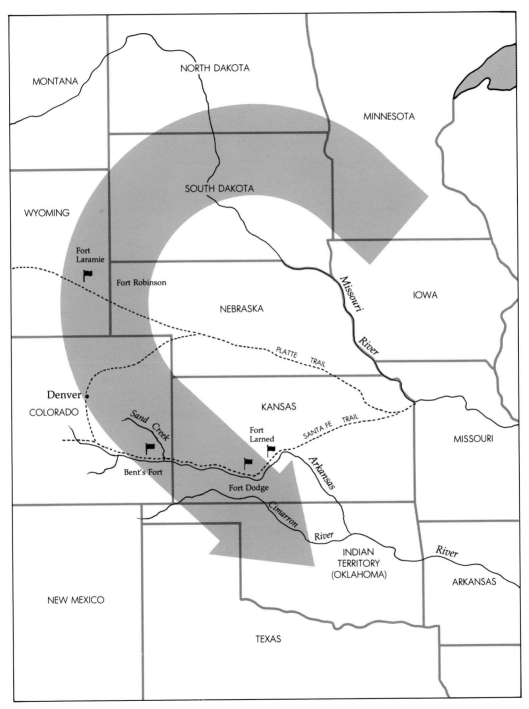

Once pioneers began to stream across the Great Plains, relations grew strained between the Cheyenne and whites.

By this time, the number of whites had risen in the Great Plains, and conflicts pitted them against the Plains Indians. In 1841, Cheyenne and Sioux clashed with a party of white trappers on the Snake River. In this fight the Indians lost 8 or 10 warriors, and 5 trappers died, including their leader. A year later, explorer John Charles Frémont encountered a Cheyenne-Arapaho village on the South Platte. As Frémont rode along the irregular path that ran through the village, he noted that before most of the lodges stood birch-limb tripods bearing glistening white shields and burnished spearheads. Frémont touched one of the shields with his gun muzzle, half expecting an angry warrior to confront him.

Yet relations between the Cheyenne and whites generally remained amicable. In 1842, the same year that Frémont visited the Cheyenne village, trader Bill Hamilton led a party into a camp of friendly Cheyenne who were willing to trade their robes and pelts for powder, balls, flints, beads, paint, blue and scarlet cloths, blankets, calico, and knives. However, dealing with white traders would eventually cause the Cheyenne great misery. ▲

In 1841, explorer John C. Fremont (shown atop the Rocky Mountains) encountered Cheyenne.

Yellow Wolf, as sketched by U.S. Army lieutenant J. S. Abert in 1845, when the two met at Bent's Fort. Albert drew likenesses of several Cheyenne.

THROUGH
THE
EYES OF WHITES

The advent of white men brought many blessings to the Cheyenne. They gladly bolstered their diet with coffee, flour, sugar, and other foods. Cheyenne women lightened their domestic burdens with household items such as pots and pans, and they enjoyed novelties such as printed cloth material, combs, mirrors, and beads. Warriors, for their part, profited from steel-bladed butcher and hunting knives, not to mention rifles and ammunition.

But the blessings were offset by deadly diseases—whooping cough, smallpox, measles, cholera, venereal infections, and, worst of all, alcoholism. Traders soon learned that Indians could easily be duped through the use of intoxicants, especially whiskey. Because liquor was new to the Indians, they had not developed a tolerance for it over centuries of use, as whites had. Many Indians loved the taste of whiskey and the happiness it induced, but it had a disastrous effect on them. For instance, in 1835, the exploring expedition of

Colonel Henry Dodge visited a Cheyenne camp near Bent's Fort and found the entire village besotted with whiskey. Men, women, and children dipped bowls and horn spoons into a large keg kept in the chief's lodge. The whiskey had been supplied by Mexican traders, who lured the inebriated Cheyenne into bartering away their robes, blankets, horses, and virtually all their worldly goods.

A thorough account of how whiskey ruined many Cheyenne was supplied by Jim Beckwourth, a mulatto frontiersman who worked as a trader for the firm of Sublette and Vasquez at its fort on the South Platte River in Colorado. In the course of his dealings he spent several years among the Cheyenne, Arapaho, Crow, and Sioux. His adventures became well known in 1856 with the publication of his autobiography. In it, Beckwourth gave an excellent description of how he and others used whiskey to swindle the Indians out of their goods.

On one occasion, Beckwourth visited the camp of chiefs Bob-tailed Horse and Old Bark. He brought 2 10-gallon kegs of whiskey, and within hours he had exchanged them for buffalo robes. This was a tremendous bargain. A well-dressed robe, the result of long and meticulous labor, fetched $5 in St. Louis. In return, the Cheyenne accepted a pint of whiskey, which cost the trader about six cents. As Beckwourth put it:

> In two hundren gallons there are one thousand six hundrend pints [*hundren* and *hundrend* are old forms of *hundred*], for each one of which the trader gets a buffalo robe worth five dollars! The Indian women toil many long weeks to dress these one thousand six hundrend robes. The white trader gets them all for worse than nothing, for the poor Indian mother hides herself and her children in the forests until the effect of the poison passes away from the husbands, fathers, and brothers, who love them when they have no whiskey, and abuse and kill them when they have.

On another occasion, Beckwourth traded 4 kegs of whiskey—some 60 gallons—for more than 1,100 robes and 18 horses, a total value of $6,000. Great as this margin of profit was, it did not satisfy most traders. Many tipped the balance more in their favor by diluting their whiskey with water to a shameful extent, usually mixing in four gallons of water for each gallon of alcohol. Others cheated by shorting the amount of liquor they put in measuring cups or by

The rakish autobiography of Jim Beckwourth, a mulatto trader, described his use of whiskey to swindle the Cheyenne.

inserting two fingers or a thumb into the cup as they poured. Some traders filled half the cup with tallow (animal fat).

Alcohol not only hurt the Cheyenne economically, it also damaged them morally. Rufus Sage, an 1841 visitor among the Sioux, Arapaho, and Cheyenne, witnessed scenes of drunken mayhem as men, women, and children raced from tipi to tipi carrying vessels of liquor and whooping and singing drunkenly. Some squirted streams of fluid from their mouths into those of others. A group of men quarreled and fought, while others staggered about in a daze or lay stretched helplessly on the ground.

PAYING THE PRICE

One of the few Cheyenne leaders to grasp the dangers of alcohol was Chief Porcupine Bear. His plea for abstinence, made to his brother-in-law Bob-tailed Horse in the mid-nineteenth century is quoted in T. D. Bonner's *The Life and Adventures of James P. Beckwourth*, published in 1931:

Once we were a great and powerful nation: our hearts were proud and our arms were strong. But a few winters ago all other tribes feared us; now the Pawnees dare to cross our hunting grounds, and kill our buffalo. Once we could beat the Crows, and, unaided, destroyed their villages; now we call other villages to our assistance, and we can not defend ourselves from the assaults of the enemy. How is this, Cheyennes: The Crows drink no whiskey. The earnings of their hunters and toils of their women are bartered to the white man for weapons and ammunition. This keeps them powerful and dreaded by their enemies. We kill buffalo by the thousand; our women's hands are sore with dressing the robes; and what do we part with them to the white trader for? We pay them for the white man's fire-water, which turns our brains upside down, which makes our hearts black, and renders our arms weak. It takes away our warriors' skill, and makes them shoot wrong in battle. Our enemies, who drink no whiskey, when they shoot, they always kill their foe. We have no ammunition to encounter our foes, and we have become as dogs, which have nothing but their teeth.

Our prairies were once covered with horses as the trees are covered with leaves. Where are they now? Ask the Crows, who drink no whiskey. When we are all drunk, they come and take them from before our eyes; our legs are helpless, and we can not follow them. We are only fearful to our women, who take up their children and conceal themselves among the rocks in the forest, for we are famishing. Our children are now sick, and our women are weak with watching. Let us not scare them away from our lodges, with their sick children in their arms. The Great Spirit will be offended at it. I had rather go to the great and happy hunting-ground now than live and see the downfall of my nation. Our fires begin to burn dim, and will soon go out entirely. My people are becoming like the Pawnees: they buy the whiskey of the trader, and, because he is weak and not able to fight them, they go and steal from his lodge.

I say, let us buy what is useful and good, but his whiskey we will not touch; let him take that away with him. I have spoke all I have to say, and if my brother wishes to kill me for it, I am ready to die. I will go and sit with my fathers in the spirit land, where I shall soon point down to the last expiring fire of the Cheyennes, and when they inquire the cause of this decline of their people, I will tell them with a straight tongue that it was the fire-water of the trader that put it out.

Sometimes these episodes culminated in extreme violence and even murder. In November 1842 the American Fur Company sent several kegs of whiskey to a Cheyenne village on Chugwater Creek, a tributary of the Platte River, in Wyoming. The alcohol, presented as a generous gift, was meant in fact to give the traders a leg up on competitors from rival companies. Its effect was tragic: The entire village became drunk and engaged in a brawl that left head chiefs Bull Bear and Yellow Lodge and six others dead.

Some chiefs recognized the danger of alcohol to the tribe's well-being. One such was Slim Face, a Southern Cheyenne chief who lived near Bent's Fort. In 1844 he resolved to confront U.S. government officials with the alcohol problem and also to inform them of the threat posed to the buffalo population by whites who were wantonly destroying the great herds. Slim Face joined a trading caravan headed for St. Louis, Missouri. His final destination was Washington, D.C., but he never made it there.

As the pioneer population grew, riverboats such as the Rosebud *made regular journeys along the Missouri River in the heart of Cheyenne territory.*

St. Louis overwhelmed Slim Face. He could not fathom how so many people could live in one village so far from the hunting grounds. He sat cross-legged on a St. Louis street corner and carved a notch in a stick each time a person passed by. Soon he had whittled the stick down to nothing. In dismay Slim Face realized he was dealing with an inexhaustible number of opponents. He gave up and returned home.

Slim Face's friend Old Wolf delighted in recounting an incident that occurred during the trip to St. Louis. At Independence, Missouri, a town along the way, Slim Face had boarded a steamboat for the first time. He was leaning against the rail that curved around the deck when the engineer's steam whistle suddenly sounded. Slim Face was so startled that he leaped into the river. He swam to safety and was given dry clothes. It was some time, however, before he could be persuaded to climb back on board. Old Wolf chided Slim Face for being frightened by something before he knew what it was. Slim Face retorted that if Old Wolf had been there, he would have jumped with him.

These years—the 1840s and 1850s—marked the final phase of largely friendly relations between the Cheyenne and whites. The problem of alcoholism aside, both groups often met on honorable terms, and time and again whites marveled at the innate nobility of the Plains Indian tribe and at the grandeur of their culture. There was little in the whites' experience that com-

In 1845, a detachment of U.S. soldiers led by Colonel S. W. Kearny met peacefully with Cheyenne living near the Platte River.

pared with the selflessness of the peace chiefs and the modesty of Cheyenne women. So impressed were many of these visitors that they felt compelled to describe what they saw and thus unwittingly helped keep alive the memory of Cheyenne culture.

Sometimes the most casual encounters provided the most intriguing insights. For instance, in 1845, Colonel Stephen Watts Kearny led a detachment of men up the Platte River and met a band of Cheyennes on the Chugwater. He found the encampment neat and "merry-looking." Hunters arrived

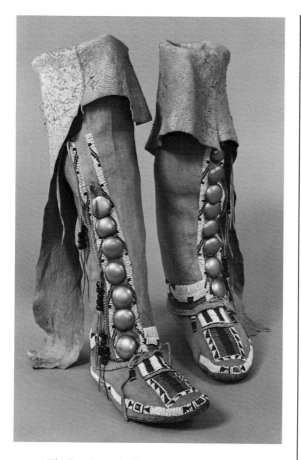

The beads and silver buttons on these boots came from white traders. In exchange they received blankets and robes that fetched a high price in St. Louis and other population centers.

with loads of buffalo meat. Women—in clothing decorated with shells, elk teeth, beads, and painted porcupine quills—sat about on buffalo robes. When one of Kearny's young officers peered closely at a Cheyenne girl to study her robe, she and her friends shrieked and giggled. They thought the officer's eyeglasses enabled him to see

through the robes to the naked flesh underneath.

In 1845, Lieutenant J. S. Abert observed Cheyennes at Bent's Fort. He sketched Yellow Wolf and met his second chief, Old Bark, who voiced regret that he could not present Abert with a pictographed robe whose drawings showed his many exploits. Abert also met Old Bark's beautiful daughter, who was courted by many suitors. They tied horses to the door of her lodge to win her hand, but she would not give up her freedom.

A more serious discovery Abert made was that the Cheyenne were still at war with the Pawnee. Once, a large Cheyenne party galloped into Bent's Fort bearing a Pawnee scalp. Chief Little Crow and his relatives—their bodies blackened with ceremonial charcoal—led the Cheyenne inside the adobe fort to celebrate their success. They were joined by blanketed, trinketed women whose faces were daubed with red and black paint. The whole band performed a Scalp Dance accompanied by singing, by the beating of tambourines, and by war whoops. Abert, sketchbook in hand, observed the celebration and drew likenesses of the participants.

Abert also witnessed a peace council that involved the Cheyenne and a group of Delaware Indians, who—having been driven from their territory in the East by white settlers—had become feared nomads in the West. In 1844 the Delaware lost 15 men in an attack by a combined force of Cheyenne and Sioux. Old Bark worried that the Delaware would seek revenge. As a peace offering, he presented the Delaware with a fine horse. The Delaware responded by inviting the Cheyenne to join many other tribes in a grand council to be held at the Salt Plains in north central Oklahoma. Both parties were satisfied and agreed to remain at peace.

Shortly after Abert's visit, two other white men stayed with the Cheyennes near the Arkansas River and gave useful accounts of what they saw. One, Englishman George Ruxton, spent time in a Cheyenne village at what the Indians called "Pretty Encampment," east of Bent's Fort. He described the camp's 50 or so tipis as arranged in rows of 10 with the chief's tipi, dyed a conspicuous red, at the center. The homes of warriors and chiefs were decorated with paintings and symbols telling stories of warfare and heroic deeds. Spears and shields were stacked before each tipi, and in front of one stood a painted pole on which several smoke-dried scalps dangled. In Ruxton's words, they "rattled in the wind like a bag of peas."

Perhaps the most remarkable account of Cheyenne life was furnished in the 1840s by Lewis Garrard, a 17-year-old from Cincinnati, who traveled to the West for health reasons. Garrard joined a trading expedition returning to Bent's Fort by way of the Santa Fe Trail. He soon found himself deep inside the world of rough-hewn mountain men and nomadic Plains Indians. At the fort he was placed under the charge of John Simpson Smith, a trader married to a Cheyenne woman. With Smith, his wife and young son as his escort, Garrard took up residence in a Cheyenne camp.

White visitors observed Cheyenne customs such as a gambling game that used dice made of bone and a basket made of willow splints and yucca leaves.

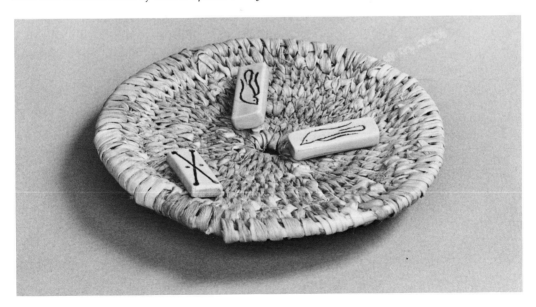

He spent the winter of 1846–47 in Cheyenne camps along the Arkansas and described what he saw in *Wah-to-yah and the Taos Trail*, a classic of the early American frontier. During his two-month stay, Garrard enjoyed the hospitality of his hosts. With them he ate meals such as buffalo jerky and dried, pounded cherries mixed with buffalo marrow. More important, he observed the activities of the camp. Garrard watched Cheyenne men sit about a winter's lodge fire conversing and smoking *kinnikinnick* (ka-nick'-ku-nick'), a blend of tobacco, bark, dried leaves, herbs, and buffalo bone marrow. He was annoyed by the men who let the women do all of the work. He admired the Cheyenne father who held his young son in his arms and sang affectionate songs to him. He shivered in sympathy as a mother bathed her son and sent him outdoors naked for airing even on the coldest winter mornings. And he learned how the Cheyenne disciplined an unruly child by pouring icy water over his head until his energy was spent and his rage quenched.

The young adventurer from Ohio carefully studied the ways of the Cheyenne. He noted their love of games and gambling and their tribal dances, performed to the beat of drums and the unending "hay-a-hay, hay-a-hay" chanted in quickening tempo as prancing warriors brandished their shields, lances, and scalp trophies. He marveled at the vermilion-painted Cheyenne girls whose brass rings and bracelets glinted with the flickering light of the bonfire.

And he described the courtship procedure wherein a boy and girl wrapped themselves together in a blanket.

Other white observers charted the changing makeup of the Cheyenne tribe. From 1825 to 1850, the rift between the groups widened. Eventually the Cheyenne became segmented into three major geographical units. The Northern Cheyenne resided west of the Black Hills, a central group ranged along the South Platte, and the Southern Cheyenne remained on the Arkansas River.

Thaddeus A. Culbertson, who explored the upper Missouri country in 1850, stated that the Cheyenne, who numbered around 3,000 people and 300 lodges, were divided into three bands: the Dog Soldier band, the Half-breed band, and the Yellow Wolf band. There were other reports of "outlaw bands" of Cheyenne who had broken apart from the main tribe and associated with neither the northern nor southern groups.

There was good reason that so many whites paid attention to the habits of the Cheyenne. The United States government had become increasingly aware of the need to establish better relations with the Indian nations of the West, to regulate trade, and to provide protection for its citizens who were streaming west in growing numbers, most of them headed for the rich farmland of the Midwest. Authorities wanted to extend American influence beyond the Mississippi River and to claim the land currently held by Mexico

(continued on page 57)

RESTLESS PEOPLE, LASTING CREATIONS

Soon after they were introduced to horses—in the mid-18th century—the Cheyenne abandoned settled village life and became nomadic hunters, pursuing deer, elk, sheep, and buffalo across the Great Plains. The meat they brought back fed the tribe, and the hides they collected supplied material that could be sewn by Cheyenne women into useful and decorative items.

This painting captures the essence of the Cheyenne horseman—a superb rider and marksman, adept with gun and bow.

Cheyenne women were remarkably resourceful, incorporating a wide array of objects—including animal teeth and bones—into their handiwork. When white traders arrived, they brought new materials, such as metal, beads, and cloth, that soon found their way onto Cheyenne designs.

A saddle blanket (opposite) from the 1840s made of buffalo hide and decorated with beads and cloth.

In a pipe bag (above right), horsehair and feathers, standard Cheyenne decorations, are fitted with metal pieces obtained from traders.

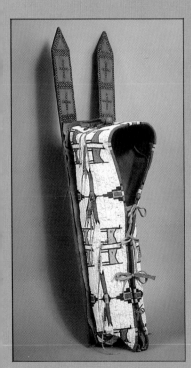

Brass tacks form crosses on this cradleboard (above).

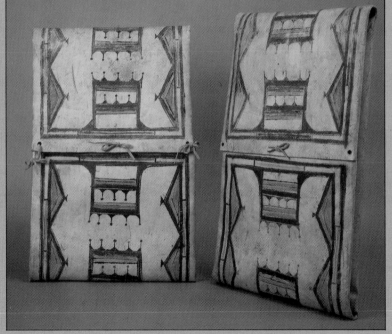

These parfleches, or storage cases, date from the 1880s. They are made of rawhide decorated with store-bought paint.

The Cheyenne excelled not only as craft workers but also as painters. For canvases they used the skin of deer, elk, and buffalo, which they covered with bold hues. Horses—usually shown in the heat of battle or during the hunt—are depicted with uncommon grace.

This hide shows mounted Cheyenne raiding a herd of wild horses.

Cheyenne horsemen battle the U.S. Cavalry in this hide painting.

This painting done in 1890 includes materials obtained from whites: a muslin canvas (softer than hide) and commercial paints.

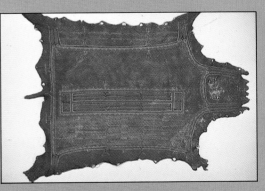

Some buffalo-hide paintings had abstract designs rather than representational figures.

This hide features traditional materials: elk skin, horsehair, and deer toes.

The painstaking job of making clothes fell to Cheyenne women. Their main material was animal hide, which they prepared with four tools: a scraper, for cleaning the hide of meat and fat; a flesher, for thinning the hide; a draw blade, for shaving off hair; and a rope, for softening the skin into workable material. This process took several days and produced the men's garments shown here.

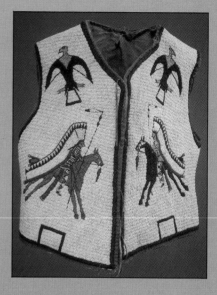

A beaded vest, made in the 1890s, features warriors and eagles, the feathers of which were prized by the Cheyenne.

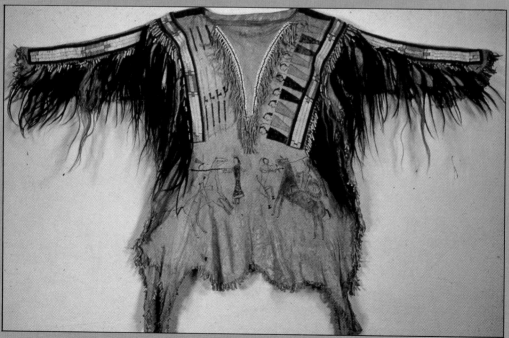

This shirt is decorated with porcupine-quill embroidery.

The fringed flaps on these high winter boots are made of deerskin. Cheyenne women often worked beads into geometric patterns. Here the blend of colors is superb.

The most common form of Cheyenne footwear was the moccasin, made of a single piece of hide folded over, with a second hide sewn on to form a thick sole. Shoes were decorated with beads and quills.

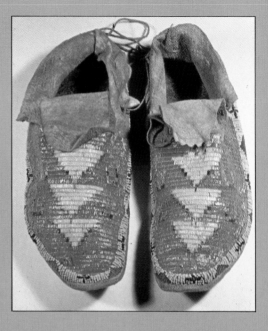

Right: *A Northern Cheyenne woman made the patterns on these moccasins with dyed quills.*

These moccasins were used in the Ghost Dance ceremony.

By the mid-19th century, large wagon trains commonly appeared on the Great Plains. The U.S. government feared for their safety and negotiated for their protection with the Cheyenne and other Indians.

(continued from page 48)

in the Southwest. As a result more treaties were initiated, forts were built, and Indian agencies were established.

In 1846 the U.S. government appointed Thomas Fitzpatrick to serve as agent for the Cheyenne and Arapaho of the upper Arkansas. Fitzpatrick had a great deal of experience with the western Indians and knew the Cheyenne from his days at the South Platte trading posts. His job was to cement good relations with the Indians and to conclude a new treaty defining their territory and securing their allegiance to the United States. Accordingly, the agent began arrangements for a great council of Plains Indians to be held in the vicinity of Ft. Laramie on the North Platte.

The Treaty of Ft. Laramie, signed on Horse Creek near the post in September 1851, was one of the spectacular events of the early West. It brought together the myriad tribal armies of the plains and mountains: Cheyenne, Arapaho, Assiniboin, Shoshone, Arikara, Gros Ventres, Mandan, Sioux, Crow, Snake, and representatives from smaller tribes. Hundreds of fully painted and feathered warriors arrived on horseback along with some 10,000 villagers whose tipis decorated the landscape.

This colorful spectacle included U.S. commissioners, who brought wagonloads of supplies and presents, escorted by blue-coated troops and accompanied by many renowned frontiersmen. One was Jim Bridger, who had personally escorted his Snake charges to the council. Another, John Simpson Smith, had lived 8 years among the Blackfeet and more than 12 among the Cheyenne. He now served as official interpreter for the Cheyenne and Arapaho.

So diverse a gathering was bound to include ancient enemies. And indeed, shortly before the council convened, a Cheyenne war party had killed and scalped a Snake man and his son on the road to Salt Lake City. The Snake contingent now demanded a settlement, and the Cheyenne agreed. An arbor made of lodge skins and poles was set up in a semicircle with one-half open on the east side. Skins and mats were arranged for seats. The Cheyenne chiefs, "as fine specimens of men as can be found anywhere," as a letter to the *Missouri Republican* noted, occupied half the seats, and the Snake and the commissioners took the other.

The session began with a long period of silence, in which everyone present smoked from a pipe—a standard Indian protocol. Then Cheyenne chief Porcupine Bear rose and made a forceful speech. He urged his young men to accept the Snake as friends, to take them by the hand, and to give them presents. He insisted that the young Cheyenne warriors should listen to the advice of the old men and not go to war without permission of the chiefs. Cheyenne elders urged the villagers to come forth.

A large copper kettle appeared, filled with boiled corn. From it a bowl was filled and passed around, each person serving himself with a ladle made from the horn of a black sheep. When the meal ended, Cheyenne chiefs made

speeches exhorting their warriors to behave themselves and make peace with the Snake. Following this, gifts were presented to the offended tribe. Each Cheyenne warrior rose to his feet, designated the recipient of his gift, and instructed his wife or child to deliver it. The recipient then embraced the bearer.

The council concluded when the Cheyennes who had killed the two Snakes returned their dried scalps. A grieving relative was consoled by assurances that the scalps had not been "danced" in celebration by the Cheyenne. He embraced the murderer, and a general whooping followed. A revelry of singing and dancing lasted through the night.

In their talks with the commissioners, the Cheyenne delegated Wan-es-sah-ta, or He Who Walks with His Toes Turned Out, to speak for them. He met with U.S. Indian superintendent D. D. Mitchell, who offered to repay the tribes for their loss of buffalo range and grassland. The treaty drawn up for the Cheyenne and Arapaho defined boundaries for their territory. Its northern and southern borders were rivers: to the north, the North Platte, which flows from Wyoming into Nebraska; to the south, the Arkansas, which runs through the lower half of Kansas, Oklahoma, and Arkansas. Its eastern border was a line through western Kansas; its western border was the Rocky Mountains. The tribes agreed to allow the United States to build roads and military posts within their territory and to recognize U.S. sovereignty.

Three great Cheyenne chiefs (left to right): White Antelope, Alights-on-the-Cloud, and Roman Nose. The first two met with President Millard B. Fillmore at the White House in 1851.

While all the assembled Indians feasted, hosted one another, and deliberated on the proposed treaty, a group of Cheyenne warriors, stripped of clothing and painted for war, presented an exhibition of horsemanship and battle maneuvers, making mock charges upon enemies with guns, lances, and bows. The display concluded with a war dance during which Cheyenne braves recounted their heroic deeds against foes.

The treaty was signed on September 17, 1851. The commission then determined that a delegation composed of representatives from all the Indian tribes should visit President Millard Fillmore in Washington, D.C. Three Cheyenne delegates were chosen: Little Chief, White Antelope, and Alights-on-the-Cloud. En route the party paused in Kansas to hold a peace council with the Pawnee before moving on to St. Louis, where they boarded a steamboat.

The Indians shrank from boarding the smoke-belching "fire horse," but soon their fears subsided, and they were delighted with the ride. In Washington, they met with President Fillmore at the White House and were taken on tours of the city. They visited local forts, naval yards, and arsenals. But they were most amazed by the Central Market and its domestic fowl hanging in rows. The Indians enjoyed the trip so much that they did not return to their homes until January 1852. They arrived at their camps filled with hope for the future. ▲

In 1863, a delegation of chiefs met with President Abraham Lincoln. Joining the chiefs for this photo in the nation's capital are interpreter John Simpson Smith, Indian agent Samuel G. Colley (far left), and Lincoln's wife, Mary (far right).

MASSACRE
ON
SAND CREEK

Like so many of the treaties Indians signed with the U.S. government, the agreement devised at Ft. Laramie created more confusion than harmony. The Indians who signed it had no inkling that their land would subsequently be invaded. Nor did they imagine that white settlers would pour into their land in large numbers. In 1853 alone—two years after the treaty was signed—15,000 whites passed through Ft. Laramie on Nebraska's Platte Trail. These intruders not only killed a great deal of game, they also brought diseases and often abused the Indians they encountered.

Similar problems developed on the Santa Fe Trail, the great transportation route along the Arkansas River. As whites flocked west, conflicts developed between them and the Indians. The first serious conflict between the Cheyenne and the U.S. Army occurred in April 1856 at a bridge on the upper Platte near what is now Laramie, Wyoming. A military officer attempted to arrest three Cheyennes for the theft of a horse. When the Cheyennes attempted to flee, one of them was killed.

Not long after this, an old trapper in the Black Hills was murdered by two Cheyennes. In June a party of Cheyenne and Arapaho attacked a pioneer wagon train on the Platte Trail, and in August some Cheyenne youths harassed and wounded a mail-wagon driver near Ft. Kearny, Nebraska. Troops from the fort responded with an attack on a Cheyenne camp, killing 10 people and wounding several more. It was inevitable that war erupt as infuriated Cheyenne warriors repeatedly struck against settlers, killing, scalping, and kidnapping. U.S. Army officers grew convinced that retaliation was necessary. In the summer of 1857 the first major military operation against the Cheyenne was undertaken, commanded by Colonel E. V. "Bull of the Woods" Sumner, a white-bearded, deep-voiced officer with a reputation as a ferocious fighter.

In 1857, Colonel E. V. Sumner defeated Cheyenne warriors in their first major skirmish with the U.S. Army.

In July, Sumner confronted a large force of Cheyenne warriors on the Republican River, which flows through southern Nebraska and Kansas. Sumner attacked with an unexpected saber charge, driving the Indians from the field. Cheyenne dead numbered between 20 and 30, but Summer's casualties were minimal: 2 men killed and 9 wounded. Thus, though their loss of warriors was not great, the Cheyenne had suffered a setback in their first major confrontation with the U.S. Army.

Further conflict arose during the Colorado gold rush, which peaked in the fall of 1859. At that time, William Bent was appointed by the U.S. government to act as Indian agent for the Cheyenne and Arapaho. Both these tribes were divided by the South Platte, half of each group living south of the river and half to the north. In December 1859 Bent reported to the superintendent of Indian affairs in St. Louis that both tribes were uneasy. They resented the invasion of gold prospectors and settlers who built such towns as Denver on their choicest land. Despite this intrusion and their displeasure with the traffic that was spoiling their hunting grounds, the Cheyenne and Arapaho continued to abide by the terms of the Ft. Laramie treaty.

In 1859 the Northern Cheyenne, along with the Sioux and Northern Arapaho, signed a treaty with Thomas S. Twiss of the North Platte Agency. The Northern Cheyenne joined the other tribes in ceding a vast area of land in western Kansas, Nebraska, and the Dakotas. In return the Cheyenne received a reservation on the Laramie River of southeastern Wyoming and were awarded a yearly payment, or annuity, of $16,000.

Meanwhile, the Southern Cheyenne and Arapaho, both destitute, petitioned the government for the region in Colorado between the Arkansas River and the Raton Mountains. According to Bent they also requested assistance in building homes and learning to raise crops. Arrangements were made to hold another treaty council with the southern bands.

On September 8, 1860, the federal commissioner of Indian Affairs, A. B. Greenwood, arrived at Bent's New Fort (erected in 1853 near Lamar, in the southeastern tip of Colorado near the Kansas border). He brought 13 wagonloads of trinkets and goods and initiated a new treaty that called for the Cheyenne to settle on a reservation immediately north of the Arkansas River. It was signed by Chiefs Black Kettle, White Antelope, Lean Bear, Little Wolf, Tall Bear, and Left Hand. Cheyenne and Arapaho tribesmen, however, objected to being confined to an arid reservation unfit either for farming or hunting. The federal government promised them food, clothing, and other goods, but the tribes preferred their traditional way of life, which revolved around the buffalo chase and horse stealing.

The Indians' objections were justified. The extremely dry summer of 1861 was very hard on the southern bands. In September they collected at Ft. Wise—located in Colorado, near Bent's Fort—and demanded the annuities promised them under the past treaties. The post commander had few supplies himself, but he distributed enough to quiet the threats being made against the fort.

Even as tensions mounted during this period, the Southern Cheyenne and Arapaho remained peaceful. Other tribes showed less restraint. The Comanche and Kiowa launched repeated raids on wagon trains traveling along the Santa Fe Trail. By spring 1863 the situation had become explosive, and newly appointed Indian agent Samuel G. Colley led a delegation of Indian chiefs to Washington, D.C. The Cheyenne sent Lean Bear, War Bonnet, and Standing in the Water to represent them.

Lean Bear spoke for the group in a meeting with President Abraham Lincoln in the East Room of the White House. John Simpson Smith interpreted for Lean Bear, who assured Lincoln the chiefs would take his advice seriously. Lean Bear explained that he longed to keep peace on the Plains but that many white men preferred war. Lincoln replied that the government shared Lean Bear's desire for peace, and he promised every effort would be made to uphold it, even if some whites violated treaty agreements. But, he observed, "It is not always possible for any father to have his children do precisely as he wishes them to do." Despite this warning, the Indian chiefs departed satisfied that Lincoln had communicated the goodwill of his nation.

Nonetheless, hostilities flared during the summer of 1863. An intoxicated Cheyenne was shot and killed by a guard at Ft. Larned in western Kansas, and rumors that Indians there planned a "war of extermination" against whites spread through Colorado. In response, territorial governor John Evans dispatched a frontiersman to contact the tribes and invite their chiefs to a peace council. But the chiefs, on a buffalo hunt in the Smoky Hill area of western Kansas, claimed they were needed by their people, many of whom were dying of whooping cough and dysentery. In addition, their horses could not manage so long a trip.

The crisis grew when some Northern Arapahos killed a family of white settlers in Denver and nearly touched off a panic. Colonel John M. Chivington, who commanded the military district of Colorado, seized on the incident as an excuse to send troops to the South Platte with instructions to "be sure you have the right ones, and then kill them." The Colorado First Cavalry attacked several Cheyenne camps in northern Colorado. More damage yet resulted from the campaign of Lieutenant George S. Eayre, who led troops from Denver into western Kansas. They followed the Republican River, intent on finding and killing Indians. On May 16, 1864, they encountered a large buffalo hunt north of Ft. Larned.

The hunt was headed by Chief Lean Bear, just back from his audience with President Lincoln. When the chief spotted the approaching troops, he and another Cheyenne rode forward to meet them. On his chest Lean Bear bore the large peace medal given him in Washington and carried a note signed by the president testifying that the chief could be trusted. It proved of no avail. As soon as the two Indians came within range, the soldiers opened fire and killed both. Eayre then scurried to the safety of Ft. Larned. This episode pushed the tribes over the brink during the summer of 1864. Kansas paid the price as Cheyenne warriors, led by the Dog Soldier band, struck with fury at wagon trains and outlying settlements.

Governor Evans issued a proclamation directing friendly Indians to appear at the various U.S. government forts. In response, Black Kettle and the

Wagon trains, such as this one (photographed during a stop at in Ft. Dodge, Kansas), became prime targets for Cheyenne raiders.

other Cheyenne leaders sent a message to Ft. Lyon. It was written by One Eye, whose daughter was married to a white man living near the Arkansas River. The commander of Ft. Lyon, Major Edward W. Wynkoop, moved by the sincerity of the Cheyenne, led an expedition to Smoky Hill, where he conducted an interview with the chiefs.

Wynkoop again was impressed by the intelligence, understanding, and candor of Chief Black Kettle. The chief, wrote Wynkoop in his memoirs, sat "calm, dignified, immovable with a slight smile on his face." Wynkoop inspired equal trust in Black Kettle. This mutual respect helped Wynkoop persuade the Cheyenne to send a delegation to Denver to meet with Governor Evans. Black Kettle made the journey, along with White Antelope and Bull Bear, a brother of Lean Bear and the leader of the Dog Soldiers.

At Denver's Camp Weld, Black Kettle made a brief but eloquent speech. He said, as the secretary of war reported to Congress, "We have come with our eyes shut, following [Wynkoop's] handful of men, like coming through the fire. All we ask is that we may have peace with the whites. You are our father; we have been travelling through a cloud; the sky has been dark ever since the war began." At this time, both Evans and Chivington were running for political office in Colorado, and their campaign tactics included pandering to the voters' anti-Indian bias. Evans openly accused the Cheyenne chiefs of initiating hostilities. Chiving-

John Evans, the territorial governor of Colorado, appealed to voters by outfitting a regiment of Indian fighters.

ton did not comment until the end of the conference, when he stated: "My rule of fighting white men or Indians is, to fight them until they lay down their arms and submit to military authority. You are nearer Major Wynkoop than any one else, and you can go to him when you get ready to do that."

Chivington's remarks implied that if the Indians came to Ft. Lyon, they would be safe. The chiefs returned to their bands and persuaded them to take that risk in order to secure peace. In November, 9 Cheyennes arrived at Ft. Lyon and reported that some 600 of their people were on their way and that 2,000 more would follow once the weather improved.

In the interim, Wynkoop, whose superiors thought him too "soft" on Indians, was relieved of his command at Ft. Lyon. His replacement was Major Scott J. Anthony. By the time Anthony took over, some 113 lodges of Arapaho—a total of 652 people—had already arrived at Ft. Lyon. They were destitute, but Anthony had no food to give them. He dispatched John Smith with instructions that the smaller group of Cheyenne, Black Kettle's band, should remain in their camp at the bend of Sand Creek north of the fort. Anthony promised they would be safe, and Black Kettle complied.

Meanwhile, other plans were under way in Denver. In August, Governor Evans secured the authority to recruit a new regiment of volunteer cavalry, the Colorado Third, whose enlistments lasted 100 days. Little use was made of the regiment, and in Denver it became known, mockingly, as the "Bloodless Third." The regiment was nearing the end of its 100-day enlistment without having fought a single battle. Feeling the pressure of political embarrassment and threatened by the recent arrival in Denver of Indian fighter General P. E. Connor, Chivington ordered the volunteer regiment to begin a march to Sand Creek. He stopped at Ft. Lyon and added its garrison to his forces.

Chivington now headed 700 troops, all armed with short-barreled carbines and pistols. His command also included 4 12-pound mountain howitzers, or cannons. The cavalry marched steadily northward in columns of four until, under a bright, starlit sky, it reached the Cheyenne encampment.

Dawn had barely broken when the troops spied the snaking tree line of Sand Creek. They next saw the tipis of Black Kettle's village, which was nestled comfortably in the crook of a large bend of Sand Creek. A range of sand hills loomed above the south bank of the bend. Beyond the village, the north bank fell away on a gradual plane, defined on the west by the course of the creek. Camp dogs barked, and the troops knew they had been seen. Without pausing Chivington immediately ordered his five battalions into action. One drove between the village and a huge horse herd grazing in the meadows to the east. Another set off to capture the herd on the back side of the bluffs south and west of the encampment.

Startled Cheyenne stumbled out of their lodges as the other Colorado units dismounted and rained rifle and pistol fire into the melee. They set up howitzers that lobbed clusters of grapeshot—small iron balls and canisters of lead and iron—into the hide-covered tipis. Among those in the camp were John Simpson Smith and the two half-Indian sons of William Bent, George and Charlie.

Cheyenne warriors fought desperately to stem the advance of the troops, and women fled with their children into the bed of Sand Creek. Black Kettle raised an American flag in order to show that his camp was friendly. The action was futile. White Antelope

A depiction of the Sand Creek Massacre in 1864. The sleeping Cheyenne had no hope of defending themselves against the U.S. Army's 700 troops.

walked forward toward his attackers with his hands held high, imploring them not to shoot. Finally he stopped in the middle of the creek bed with his arms folded and was killed. Once the camp was routed, the troops pursued the fleeing figures, shooting or hacking them down with sabers. A group of women and children tried to hide in a cut in the river bank, but they were discovered by soldiers who had great sport picking off their victims one by one.

By 3:00 P.M. the shooting had ceased, and the troops began looting the village. Some of the 100-day volunteers took scalps. John Simpson Smith escaped harm, but his half Indian son Jack was captured and murdered; his corpse was harnessed to a horse and dragged around the campsite. Black Kettle and his wife managed to escape. The bodies on the battlefield included those of One Eye and Arapaho chief Left Hand.

In his report, Chivington claimed that 400 to 500 Indians had been killed, compared with a loss to his own forces of 9 killed and 38 wounded. He tried to glorify the Sand Creek Massacre by referring to it not as a slaughter but as "one of the most bloody Indian battles ever fought on these plains." ▲

Bull Bear led the Dog Soldiers, the most feared of the Cheyenne military societies.

LOSING
BATTLES

As Black Kettle and his band of elders, women, and children fled south of the Arkansas, Cheyenne drums summoned warriors to the headwaters of the Republican River. Chivington's betrayal and massacre of the peaceful band of Southern Cheyenne at Sand Creek had catapulted the military societies, particularly the Dog Soldiers, to great power within the tribe, and at the meeting furious war leaders exhorted some 2,000 Cheyenne, Arapaho, and Sioux fighters to "make war to the knife" against the whites.

From camps in Kansas and Colorado, the Cheyenne mounted assaults against travelers and frontier settlements. In January 1865 they staged a well-organized strike on Ft. Rankin on the South Platte trail near the small settlement of Julesburg, Colorado. First a war party attacked a wagon train near the fort, killing 12 men. Next, the Cheyenne drew a company out of the fort and massacred every man. Then they overran the defenseless settlement,

burning buildings, looting, and making off with as much plunder as their horses could carry.

Many Southern Cheyenne bands moved northward to the protection of the Black Hills, and—as they crossed the Platte—fought an indecisive battle with troops from Ft. Laramie, Wyoming. In April 1865, Cheyenne were said to have visited the Sioux north of the Black Hills and to have incited them to join their war against the U.S. Army. Meanwhile, sporadic attacks against settlers continued along both the Platte and Arkansas trails. Sometimes they were the doing of the Cheyenne and Arapaho, sometimes of the Comanche and Kiowa. Both groups raided wagon trains, stole horses, killed and scalped civilians, plundered stagecoach stations, and destroyed telegraph lines.

The American government was divided in its response. The army prepared for a punitive campaign against the Indians in western Kansas, but Comanche-Kiowa agent Jesse Leavenworth pushed for a new peace council and new treaties. He sent Jesse Chisholm, a frontiersman and trader, on a trip southward into Indian Territory to persuade the Comanche and the Kiowa to participate. Intermediaries also contacted Black Kettle, then camped on Wolf Creek in northwestern Oklahoma. Despite threats by the Dog Soldiers that their horses would be killed, Black Kettle, George Bent, and their families attended a council held at the mouth of the Little Arkansas River (the site of what is now Wichita, Kansas). There, in early August, the Indians agreed to appear at yet another peace council, this time in October.

The council included a wide range of famous men of the frontier, representing both the Indians and the federal government. Frontiersmen such as Kit Carson and William Bent attended, as did James Steele, who represented the Bureau of Indian Affairs (BIA), the federal agency founded in 1824 and recognized by Congress 10 years later. Also present were Leavenworth, Chisholm, John Simpson Smith, and many other Western notables.

In his opening speech to the commission, Black Kettle stated the grievances of Indians who desired peace. "Your young soldiers—I don't think they listen to you," he said. "You bring presents, and when I come to get them I am afraid they will strike me before I get away. When I come in to receive presents I take them up crying. Although wrongs have been done me I live in hopes. I have not got two

hearts." Then he added: "My shame is as big as the earth. . . . I once thought that I was the only man that persevered to be the friend of the white man, but since they have come and [robbed] our lodges, horses and everything else, it is hard for me to believe white men any more."

The Treaty of the Little Arkansas granted the Cheyenne and Arapaho a new reservation area on the Cimarron River. In exchange, they gave up their last tribal claim to lands in Colorado. Black Kettle and a few other Cheyenne and Arapaho chiefs signed the treaty, but they represented only a small portion of the southern bands. The Dog Soldiers and other warrior groups had no intention of forsaking their buffalo hunting grounds in western Kansas. During the winter of 1865–66, Cheyenne warrior bands killed and scalped several people, burned stagecoach and railroad stations, and harassed transport wagons.

Major General Winfield Scott Hancock, newly assigned as military commander in Kansas, threatened a retaliatory war if the Cheyenne did not surrender to him those guilty of the crimes committed along the Smoky Hill River in Kansas. In March 1867 Hancock departed Ft. Riley, Kansas, with 1,400 infantry, artillery, cavalry, scouts, wagon drivers, and others, who all marched to Ft. Larned. Hancock's subordinate, Lieutenant Colonel George Armstrong Custer, who was to become world famous, commanded the U.S. Seventh Cavalry.

In 1866, Major Winfield Scott Hancock, the military commander of Kansas, threatened a large-scale war against the Cheyenne.

After a brief delay caused by a late-spring blizzard, a meeting with the chiefs of a large village of Cheyenne and Sioux was arranged by Wynkoop, who had become an Indian agent. Hancock exercised little diplomacy. He curtly told the Indians that if they did not behave at the meeting they would be killed. He then ordered his army to advance toward the Indian camp. They were met by a large force of Cheyenne and Sioux drawn up in a battle line. Violence was averted when Wynkoop rode forward with a white truce flag. When Hancock entered the camp the next morning he was enraged to learn that during the night the Indians, fearing another Sand Creek, had fled, leaving their tipis behind.

Hancock ordered Custer to pursue them. He did so, following a confusing trail that frequently forked off to both the left and the right. Custer doggedly hewed to the middle course until finally it faded away into the prairie of western Kansas. Meanwhile Hancock burned the tipis and equipage of the village, an act that further fueled the anger and distrust of the Cheyenne.

During the summer, Plains Indians committed more raids on Smoky Hill, so Custer led another campaign through the sparse country of northwestern Kansas. Again his efforts proved futile. He met the enemy only once, and his troops were outmaneuvered by a Sioux party under Pawnee Killer. The Sioux chief was believed to be responsible later for the deaths of Lieutenant Lyman Kidder, 10 cavalrymen, and a Sioux scout whose mutilated corpses were discovered by Custer's troops.

For their part, the Cheyenne continued to hamper American expansion and commerce in the plains. Authorities still debated over how best to deal with them. White settlers in Kansas joined the army in demanding a punitive war, whereas Indian Bureau "olive branchers" urged another peace effort. The U.S. government chose this second approach, and Congress voted funds for a peace commission to draw up another treaty with the southern tribes.

This time Leavenworth himself journeyed to the Salt Fork of the Arkansas, in northern Oklahoma, to persuade the Comanche and Kiowa to attend still another treaty council in 1867. Other couriers traveled to the camps of the Cheyenne and Arapaho on Wolf Creek. Finally, it was arranged for a grand council to be held that autumn on Medicine Lodge Creek in the extreme south of Kansas.

The meeting began with the tribes involved—the Cheyenne, Arapaho, Comanche, Kiowa, and Plains Apache—all airing their grievances. Presents were then distributed by the peace commission, which had no difficulty signing new agreements with each tribe, except the Cheyenne. Black Kettle and his peace faction willingly granted new concessions, but the stubborn Dog Soldiers refused to join the proceedings. Instead, they made the commission wait while they conducted their rite of Renewal of the Medicine Arrows.

When they finally arrived, the Dog Soldiers showed open disdain for the council, but eventually they were persuaded to sign the treaty. It relegated them to a reservation area along the Salt Fork of the Arkansas River in the Indian Territory (now Oklahoma). The band agreed to go there only after a member of the commission made an unofficial spoken commitment that contradicted the written terms of the treaty by saying that the Cheyenne would be permitted to hunt buffalo north of the Arkansas River. This false assurance on a key issue would ultimately doom the Treaty of Medicine Lodge.

Even if the treaty's contradictions had been cleared up, problems between the Cheyenne and whites would have persisted. Westward expansion had become the rallying cry of American policy, and the stubborn presence of the Cheyenne in western Kansas alarmed settlers who were pushing into the country. Anti-Indian feeling in the state peaked when a war party consisting of Cheyenne, Arapaho, and Sioux made a raid upon some Kansas settlements. The warriors had intended to raid a Pawnee village, but instead they had gotten drunk and attacked frontier outposts along the Saline and Solomon rivers. They committed murder and rape and carried off captives.

Demands for retaliation rang out loudly through the territory. In response, General Philip H. Sheridan, the military commander in Kansas, authorized the formation of a special unit of white frontiersmen under Colonel George A. Forsyth. Sheridan reasoned that a small team of scouts, unencumbered by the heavy equipment of a larger military force, would have better luck ferreting out the Indians. Forsyth plunged into the Indian country west of Ft. Wallace. He was accompanied by some 50 mounted scouts, who discovered signs of Indian presence as they proceeded up the Republican River. After going into camp on the evening of September 16, the party saw an Indian signal fire on a distant hill.

The following dawn, while the scouts' coffeepots still sat on the fire, the Cheyennes struck. Several warriors rushed at the troops' horses, waving blankets and war whooping. Hundreds

This woodcut, made in 1865, shows Cheyenne attacking a pioneer wagon train. Unexpected raids of this sort sent terror through the Plains.

more appeared from all directions, sounding their battle cry and firing as they surged forward. The scouts fled to a sandbar on the river and were pinned down there. They held off numerous charges, some led by the great Cheyenne warrior Roman Nose. He made a magnificent sight as he guided his men down the riverbed against the sandbar fortification, his gorgeous, feathered headdress trailing behind. During one such assault, however, a bullet from a scout ended his life.

For nine days the scouts were besieged and held to the sandbar, enduring sniper fire, severe hunger, and the stench of their dead horses. Several of their party perished, including surgeon John Mooers and Lieutenant Fred Beecher, nephew of the noted New York preacher Henry Ward Beecher. Forsyth himself was badly wounded at the onset of the fight but survived until a rescue column arrived on September 25. At the same time that these Cheyenne quashed Forsyth's forces, the bands who had taken refuge below the Arkansas River repulsed an inept venture into northwestern Indian Territory by General Alfred Sully.

These botched military efforts convinced Sheridan that catching and defeating the fleet-ponied Plains Indian warriors on the open prairie was next to impossible. He concluded that it would be necessary to strike the Indians in their home camps with a winter's campaign.

Other elements of the U.S. government were still trying to work out amicable relations with the Indians. Even as Sheridan was formulating his plans, the U.S. government reactivated previously abandoned Ft. Cobb in Oklahoma as an Indian agency. It was now to become an Indian sanctuary. General William B. Hazen was appointed to supervise the issuance of goods and supplies to peaceful tribes seeking refuge there.

As winter approached, the Cheyenne under Black Kettle and Little Robe withdrew even deeper to the south, camping in western Oklahoma near the Antelope Hills, where they joined Arapaho, Comanche, Kiowa, and Plains Apache. On November 20, Black Kettle led a party of Cheyenne and Arapaho to Ft. Cobb for talks with Hazen. He told the officer that his band of 180 lodges, then encamped on the Washita River, wished for peace and were willing to move to Ft. Cobb. Hazen rejected the plea. He stated that he lacked the authority to make peace and warned the chiefs that Sheridan's troops were coming to fight them. The chiefs returned to their camps. Black Kettle's band of 50 tipis was now the farthest west of the winter camps of some 6,000 other Indians.

On the night of November 26, Black Kettle convened a meeting of his band's elders at his lodge to discuss their situation. They had been denied access to Ft. Cobb, Sheridan was on their trail, and they needed to decide on a plan of action. One man told of a big troop con-

General William B. Hazen, the commanding officer at Oklahoma's Ft. Cobb, denied Black Kettle's band asylum there but warned the chief that Sheridan's troops were after him.

tingent seen by a Kiowa war party in the snowy north of the Canadian River. Some scoffed at the idea that "bluecoats" would be out in such cold weather. Others felt they were far enough south to be safe from attack. They all agreed, however, that they should move their camp downriver the following day.

Their danger was much greater than the Cheyenne elders realized. Sheridan had planned a three-pronged winter

SEVENTH CAVALRY CAMPAIGN AREA 1867–69

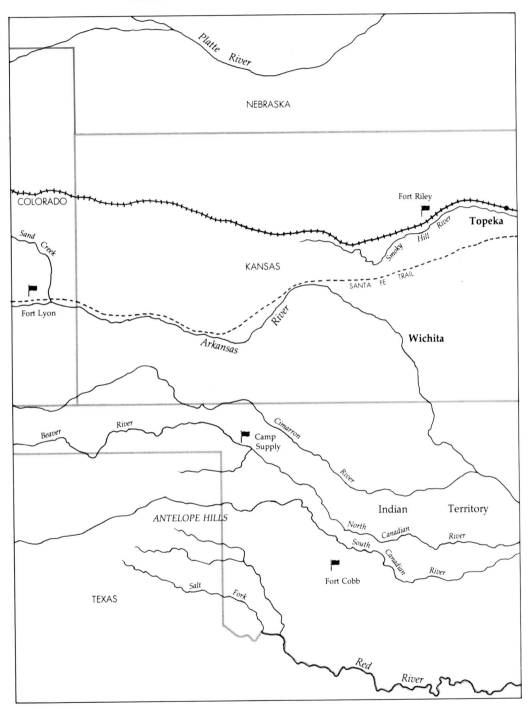

campaign into Oklahoma. His main force, from Ft. Dodge, Kansas, would be joined by forces sent down from Ft. Lyon, Colorado, and eastward from Ft. Bascom, New Mexico. The main command had already reached the juncture of Beaver and Wolf creeks on November 18 and set about erecting temporary quarters named Camp Supply.

Five days later, in a howling snowstorm, the Seventh Cavalry, led by Custer, marched southwest down Wolf Creek in search of Indians. After turning south to the Antelope Hills a scouting party of the expedition discovered an Indian trail heading across the snow-covered prairie toward the Washita River. Leaving his wagons and making a forced march throughout the starlit night of November 26, 1868, Custer located and surrounded an Indian village nestled in a bend of the Washita.

It was Black Kettle's band—the remnants of the same band that had been massacred at Sand Creek by Chivington. On November 27, 1864—almost four years to the day after Sand Creek—Custer attacked at dawn. Just as they had four years earlier, the Cheyenne awoke to the sounds of bugles, gunfire,

This woodcut of Camp Supply, in northwest Oklahoma, appeared in Harper's Weekly *in 1869, at about the time that starving Southern Cheyenne bands surrendered at the fort.*

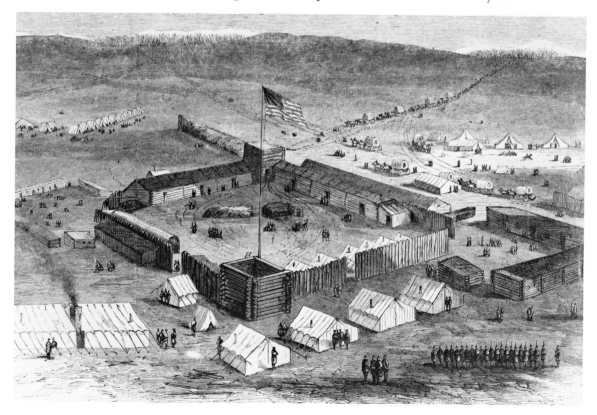

and whooping cavalrymen charging pell-mell into their village. Once again the slaughter was merciless. Indian men, women, and children were cut down by bullets and sabers as they fled for their lives. Among them were the great peacemaker Black Kettle and his wife, both killed as they attempted to wade across the Washita on a single horse.

After burning the Cheyenne's lodges, robes, clothing, food, and saddles and shooting their horses, Custer found himself surrounded by warriors from the villages downriver. In a letter to the *New York Times*, Frederick Benteen described them as "savages on flying steeds, with shields and feathers gay . . . circling everywhere, riding like devils incarnate." During the battle an improvised detachment under Major Joel Elliott had disappeared in pursuit of Cheyenne. They had not been seen since. But with Indians swarming the hills about him, Custer realized he was cut off from the supply train he had left behind at the Antelope Hills. He regrouped his forces and feigned a march farther downstream toward the Indian camps. Then, under cover of darkness, he turned about and retreated to Camp Supply, taking as captives several Cheyenne women and children.

Days later, Sheridan led his army back to the battlefield where the corpses of missing troopers were found along with the bodies of civilians captured previously on the Santa Fe Trail. Sheridan then proceeded to Ft. Cobb and set up headquarters while his other

forces—from New Mexico and Colorado—scoured the Texas panhandle for Indians.

In January 1869 Sheridan established a new military post in Oklahoma, at Ft. Sill, near the Wichita Mountains on Medicine Bluff Creek. Custer and his Seventh Cavalry, which had been joined at Camp Supply by the 19th Kansas Volunteer Cavalry Regiment, remained at this fort until March 2. On his return march to Kansas, Custer took a circuitous route into the Texas panhandle in an attempt to rescue two white women who were known to be held captive by the Cheyenne.

After a grueling march, Custer's scouts finally found an Indian trail that led them to a Cheyenne camp on the Sweetwater River just west of the 100th meridian, the line that marked the Texas boundary. Custer, his forces badly worn out and in disarray, received a friendly greeting from Cheyenne chief Medicine Arrows. Through Mo-na-se-tah, an Indian girl whom he had taken captive on the Washita, Custer learned that the two white women, taken in Kansas during the previous summer, were being held in the Cheyenne camp.

Custer lured the Cheyenne chiefs to his camp and then took three of them hostage. He threatened to hang them if the two women were not released. Eventually Anna Morgan and Sarah White, wearing only flour sacks, were brought in. Custer, however, reneged on his promise to release the three Cheyenne captives. Instead he took them with him as he and his command marched back to Kansas via Camp Supply, leaving the southern bands of the Cheyenne scattered upon the prairie, severely weakened. But the fighting spirit of the Cheyenne warrior societies was far from dead.

At the same time that chiefs Little Robe, Minimic, and others met with Colonel Benjamin Grierson at Ft. Sill and agreed to settle on a reservation in the Camp Supply vicinity, 165 tipis of Dog Soldiers, led by Tall Bull and White Horse, headed north to join the Sioux on the Republican River in western Kansas. There they were attacked by troops under the command of Major E.

A. Carr. The Cheyenne put up a stout resistance before fleeing, leaving 25 dead warriors on the field.

Once again the Dog Soldiers launched retaliatory raids against settlements, wagon transports, and outposts of the Kansas Pacific Railroad, each time taking prisoners. Carr followed in pursuit. In July 1869, guided by Pawnee scouts under the command of Frank and Luther North, he located Tall Bull's village north of the Platte River at Summit Springs. Carr struck forcefully, and in a hard, day-long fight, 52 Cheyennes—including Tall Bull—were killed, and their entire village and belongings destroyed. The

These women and children were taken captive by George Armstrong Custer at the Battle of Washita River in 1868.

Ft. Sill, Oklahoma, in about 1890, two decades after Cheyenne chiefs Little Robe and Minimac met there with Colonel Benjamin Grierson and agreed to settle on a reservation.

survivors staggered away and sought refuge among the Sioux on the White River.

The defeat of Tall Bull's band ended Cheyenne residence in the country between the Platte and the Arkansas. This land of western Kansas and eastern Colorado, once the stronghold of the Cheyenne Dog Soldiers, had now been wrested away by whites for their stage routes, railroads, forts, and settlements. The Dog Soldiers—the scourge of the Plains—disbanded. Some went north and others remained south of the Arkansas River.

Meanwhile, the starving southern bands made their way to Camp Supply and placed themselves at the mercy of the U.S. government for food and shelter. There they would be under the guardianship of members of the Quakers, the Society of Friends, to whom President Ulysses S. Grant had been persuaded by peace proponents to assign the management of the nation's Indian tribes. ▲

U.S. Army general George Armstrong Custer sat for this portrait by Mathew Brady in about 1870.

7

THE
LAST
STAND

The reservation area assigned to the Cheyenne and Arapaho by the Treaty of Medicine Lodge in 1867 was situated in north central Oklahoma. It was a poor location. The water there—supplied by the Salt Fork of the Arkansas River—was too brackish for the Indians and their ponies, and the area was much too accessible to Osage horse thieves who lived nearby. The new Cheyenne agent, Brinton Darlington, a Quaker, eventually moved their agency south to the central Oklahoma area along the North Canadian River, near El Reno. This site soon became known as the Darlington Agency. President Grant then issued an executive order that gave the Cheyenne and Arapaho a new reservation area containing more than 4 million acres and extending west to the Texas panhandle.

Darlington was well into his sixties when he was appointed agent to the Southern Cheyenne and Arapaho, but he had the energy and hope of a younger man. He busily erected agency buildings—a school for Indian children in addition to offices, a dormitory, barns, stables, storehouses, and housing for himself and his staff. He also built a sawmill and broke land to make way for corn fields and vegetable gardens. Like the other Quaker agents who arrived in the Indian Territory, Darlington vowed to prove that the "Indian problem" could be handled peacefully.

Many impediments hampered his efforts. White traders still sneaked whiskey into Indian camps. Hunters descended on the great buffalo herds, destroying the tribe's prime game. Horse thieves—most of them white men—preyed upon Cheyenne herds. U.S. Army officers, resentful of the presence of the Quakers, opposed them at every turn. The toughest obstacle was posed by the Indians themselves, who balked at Quaker efforts to introduce their children to formal schooling and to turn proud hunters into farmers. Such leaders as Bull Bear and Medicine

Stone Calf and his wife posed for this picture in 1877, about 10 years after he led a small band into the Darlington Agency.

Arrows adamantly refused to bring their people into the new agency. Eventually, Stone Calf arrived with 13 lodges, accompanied by John Simpson Smith and George Bent and their Cheyenne families.

Yet the majority of the Southern Cheyenne remained afield, plagued both by hunger and diseases such as whooping cough and scarlet fever. Many children died during the winter of 1870–71. Cheyenne warriors joined in raiding parties against settlers in Texas and Kansas, and there was much talk of a new war.

Darlington died of natural causes in the spring of 1872. His fragile legacy of peace lasted through the year. The following winter, the Cheyenne managed to find and kill many buffalo and thus had enough to eat. But other problems persisted. Cheyenne women objected when their robes, the result of long, laborious effort, ended up in the hands of swindlers who duped Cheyenne men with whiskey. Pushed beyond the limit of their tolerance, the women refused to skin, tan, and sew any more hides into robes. This may have been the first sit-down strike in the American West.

In Kansas, the Cheyenne learned that the first sign of trouble from whites was the arrival of government surveyors, who measured and mapped the land for railroads and settlement. The Indians knew well that the surveyors' presence paved the way for white homesteaders who took away land that was rightfully theirs. They became fair game for Cheyenne warriors, and in the spring of 1873, a surveying party was massacred by Cheyenne near Camp Supply. Knowing that army retaliation was inevitable, Cheyenne war factions led by Gray Beard, Bull Bear, Medicine Arrows, and others retreated to the upper Washita.

The following autumn, agent John D. Miles tried to calm the situation by taking a group of chiefs to Washington. But even as they made their journey, a

160-man Cheyenne war party invaded Colorado, spoiling for a fight with the Ute Indians living there. The frontier violence continued into 1874. Even the Darlington Agency was threatened, and some of its stock was run off by Cheyenne. After three settlers were slain near Medicine Lodge, Kansas, other homesteaders fled to safety.

In June 1874 a U.S. military detachment battled a party of Cheyenne and Kiowa above Camp Supply, and a party of white buffalo hunters was attacked near Adobe Walls in the Texas panhandle. Two of the hunters died. Later in the month, a combined force of Comanche, Kiowa, Arapaho, and Cheyenne surrounded the hunters' refuge in the ravine-slashed country of the Canadian River and made an unsuccessful attempt to overwhelm the makeshift fort. The Cheyenne lost six men in what became known as the Battle of Adobe Walls.

The next month, warriors struck a wagon train transporting goods north of the Darlington Agency. Three teamsters were shot and killed, and freighter Patrick Hennessey was tied to a wagon wheel and burned to death. In August another surveying party was wiped out near Ft. Dodge, Kansas.

The string of incidents proved a boon to General Sheridan, who could now argue effectively that Quaker appeasement policies had failed. The federal government gave him permission to plan a punitive campaign against the tribes. He devised a five-prong attack. It included fighting units that set out

In 1874, Colonel Nelson A. Miles subdued a large Cheyenne force in the Texas Panhandle and burned several villages.

from Ft. Union in New Mexico, Ft. Concho in Texas, Camp Supply, and Ft. Sill. A final unit also drove westward between the latter two.

In August Colonel Nelson A. Miles led a force on a southwestern march into the Texas panhandle. There it subdued a large Cheyenne party and burned a few scattered villages before retiring from the area. A month later, another column of cavalry and infantry—led by Colonel Ranald S. Mackenzie—pushed south into the Texas panhandle and staged a surprise attack on a large village of combined tribes on the floor of the Palo Duro Canyon. Most of the inhabitants escaped, but Mackenzie destroyed some 400 lodges along with food supplies. He captured 1,400 Indian horses.

A still larger encampment was struck by forces under the command of Lt. Colonel George P. Buell, who destroyed 500 tipis and seized a great many ponies. The other prongs of Sheridan's campaign failed to engage the Indians in major battles, though eventually the Ft. Sill column, under Lt. Colonel J. W. Davidson, destroyed 50 Cheyenne lodges in the hills along the Red River.

Throughout 1874 Sheridan's army continued to harass the Cheyenne. The troops killed few tribesmen, but they pushed families to the brink of starvation, destroyed their homes, and depleted their all-important pony herds and ammunition supplies. The Cheyenne could no longer hide, and by year's end many had surrendered.

In March 1875 the last 821 holdouts came into Darlington. Most turned in their arms, but several secretly held on to their rifles. Conflict arose when American troops tried to place some Cheyenne chiefs and warriors in leg irons. A young warrior named Black Horse rebelled and tried to escape. Guards gunned him down. Other Cheyenne fired back and retreated to a sand hill near the agency. There they held off the troops until nightfall, when they fled north.

Some were intercepted and killed by U.S. troops on the Smoky Hill River of western Kansas. Most of the others were eventually rounded up again, and the military resumed its plan to punish the war leaders. Thirty-one men and a woman were selected, placed in irons, and shipped by railway car to prison at Ft. Marion, Florida. One of them, Chief Gray Beard, was shot and killed en route when he jumped off the train and made an attempt to escape.

Thus concluded the last major outbreak by the Southern Cheyenne. Their reign over the prairie was ended, their days of wild freedom gone forever. They were now at the mercy of the U.S. government.

The Northern Cheyenne, however, had not given up the fight. They loved the high country of the upper Missouri River. They felt spiritually linked to the beautiful mountains and valleys cut by bubbling icy-watered streams and teeming with bear, elk, caribou, and other wild game. It pained the Northern Cheyenne that these natural beauties and resources were threatened by white intruders. First came the multitude of immigrants who crossed their land on the way to Utah, California, and Oregon. Next came forts and soldiers. Then, in the 1860s, gold was discovered in western Montana, and prospectors flooded into territory where the Sioux, Northern Arapaho, and Northern Cheyenne hunted and camped. The Indians suffered again in 1866, when the U.S. government

Chief Minimac was one of 31 Cheyennes shipped by rail to the prison in Ft. Marion, Florida, in 1875.

opened three new forts on the Bozeman Trail, which cut north from Colorado through Wyoming into Montana.

Northern Cheyenne warriors joined the Sioux leader Red Cloud, who attacked the forts as well as the transports that traveled between them. On December 21, 1866, the allied tribes laid siege to Ft. Phil Kearny, located on the Powder River just east of the Big Horn Mountains in northern Wyoming. Two Northern Cheyenne chiefs, Little Wolf and Dull Knife (or Morning Star), served as war leaders.

For some time the Indians had been attacking small groups near the fort and making off with horses and cattle.

When troops left the fort to search for them, the war parties always retreated. Their purpose was to lure troops into a trap, where a large warrior force could attack them. They repeated this pattern until one morning when a sizable woodcutting detachment, traveling in several wagons, emerged from the fort. Little Wolf and Dull Knife sent a small war party to waylay it. The wagon train drew into a defensive circle until more troops from the fort arrived. The detachment then proceeded on toward the piney woods.

At the same time, another Indian party, mounted on swift ponies, attacked the wagon train and then retreated into the nearby hills, hotly pursued by the troops. The soldiers followed—into an ambush. A much larger force of Indians set upon them and forced the troops to dismount and fight on foot. All 81 soldiers, led by Lieutenant W. J. Fetterman, were killed.

The Fetterman Massacre, as it became known, spurred the U.S. government to make new peace overtures to the northern tribes. In 1868 the U.S. agreed to abandon the forts on the Bozeman Trail and withdraw its troops. Two new agencies, Spotted Tail and Red Cloud, were established for the Indians. Both were ultimately located on the White River of South Dakota. The Northern Cheyenne rejected any attempt to place them on a reservation and continued to roam about the Yellowstone and Big Horn country of northern Wyoming. Occasionally they visited Sioux and Gros Ventres at the agencies, but mostly they wandered, hunted, and raided the Crow and Shoshone as they had in the old days.

By 1873 the membership rolls at the Red Cloud Agency, prepared by the Bureau of Indian Affairs, listed 1,900 Northern Cheyenne. The government planned to move them to Oklahoma, where the Southern Cheyenne were located. But Northern Cheyenne leaders—Little Wolf, Dull Knife, and others—balked. They loved their homeland, they said, and preferred to die there rather than to leave it. In November 1873 a delegation of Northern Cheyenne went to Washington, D.C., for an interview with President Grant. Grant told them that the treaty they had signed in 1868 forced them to accept the move south. He was wrong: The treaty did not commit the tribe to move; it only expressed the desire of the U.S. that

General George Custer and Indian scouts gather outside his tent. When this photograph was taken—in the early 1870s—Custer's troops were assigned to protect the construction of the Union Pacific Railroad.

they do so. The chiefs had never agreed to it. In consequence, the Northern Cheyenne were able to resist deportation for the time being.

The following year, General Custer led an exploratory expedition into the Black Hills, an area in the Dakotas long considered a sanctuary by the Cheyenne, Arapaho, and Sioux. Not only did Custer's incursion incense the tribes, it led to the discovery of gold and an ensuing rush there by white miners in 1875. A number of prospectors and others were killed by Indians.

The government tried to purchase the Black Hills, but the tribes spurned their offers, and in the spring of 1876 the U.S. War Department drew up plans to contain and punish the tribes residing along the Yellowstone River. A three-strike campaign was conceived: General George Crook, a renowned Indian fighter, moved northwest from newly built Ft. Fetterman, in Wyoming; General John Gibbon headed southeast from Ft. Shaw, in Montana; and General Alfred Terry proceeded west from Ft. Abraham Lincoln, in South Dakota.

On May 29 Crook left Ft. Fetterman with 15 troops of cavalry and 5 companies of infantry. They marched along the Tongue River, where on June 9 a war party attacked them. The party was small and easily repulsed, but another, more severe engagement with Northern Cheyenne and Sioux occurred a few days later at the head of the Rosebud River in southeastern Montana. Neither side prevailed, but Crook had to turn back in order to regroup his troops.

The Cheyenne and Sioux warriors returned to camps on the Little Bighorn and held war dances. Meanwhile, General Terry had begun his push westward from Ft. Abraham Lincoln. He took his infantry force up the Yellowstone by steamboat and sent the Seventh Cavalry, under the command of Custer, to scout overland. Custer had very nearly lost his post because of political disagreements with President Grant.

The two forces rejoined at the mouth of the Rosebud River. Custer conferred with Terry aboard the steamboat *Far West* and was ordered to follow a broad Indian trail that wound along the Rosebud. At noon on June 22, Custer began his march with about 600 troopers, 44 Indian scouts, and 20 or so packers (who carried supplies), guides, and civilians. Tom Custer, the general's brother, commanded C Company, while another brother, Boston Custer, came along as packmaster—a civilian role.

On June 24 Custer reached a point where the Indian trail veered abruptly away from the Rosebud and snaked westward toward the Little Bighorn valley. Custer followed this trail, making camp that night on a ridge that divided the Rosebud and the Little Bighorn. The next morning, his scouts observed smoke in the valley ahead.

Though Custer surmised that a sizable Indian camp was situated there, he had no inkling of the strength of the Sioux and Cheyenne forces. He did not know they had pushed Crook back; nor was he aware that some 12,000 to 15,000 Indians—including about 5,000 well-armed warriors—lay in wait for him. The majority of these forces were Sioux, but at the upper end of the camp was a fighting force of Northern Cheyenne bolstered by Southern Cheyenne warriors who had fled their reservation in Indian Territory.

In the past, Custer had been unable to pin down Plains Indians—as he approached, they would vanish on their fast ponies. He now saw an opportunity to defeat them in pitched battle and feared that any delay would enable them to escape from the valley. He violated his orders to await Terry and attacked. He divided his command into three battalions, placing three companies under Major Marcus Reno, three more under Captain Frederick Benteen, and leading the remainder of the troops himself, except for one company that stayed in the rear to protect the pack train.

Benteen's battalion was dispatched to the left of the trail to scout, and Custer and Reno continued toward the Little Bighorn. About two miles from the river, a portion of the Indian village came into view. Quickly, without scouting the enemy camps or surveying the lay of the land, Custer ordered Reno to cross the river and charge the lower end of the camp. He then led his own troops along the east bank of the Little Bighorn, which was severely cut with gullies. His strategy was to support Reno's attack by assaulting the flank and rear of the Indian stronghold.

Custer, accompanied by his personal aide and his bugler, rode to the top of a hill and lifted his field glasses to his eyes. He gazed down on several hundred tipis—only a portion of the village. He turned in his saddle and waved his hat to Reno's forces, who were charging hard on the south end of the camp. Before riding back to his command, Custer spoke to his aide, who quickly scribbled a note. This man handed it to the bugler and ordered him to rush it to Benteen, who was still scouring the country behind them. The note read: "Benteen. Come on. Big village. Be quick. Bring packs. P.S. Bring packs." The bugler hurried to the rear, noting as he passed that Reno's men had charged the village and engaged the Indians across the river. Reno, it turned out, had met far more resistance than anticipated. Before him swarms of Indians rose out of the grass, firing rifles. When his cavalry charge faltered, Reno ordered his men to dismount and fight on foot. But the number of Indians steadily increased, and Reno had his men remount and retreat to the shelter of the bluffs across the river.

Shortly after 3:00 P.M., Custer's bugler located Benteen, whose horses had struggled through the rough terrain. Benteen now pushed forward rapidly, joining Reno just as the latter's battalion, depleted and unnerved, reached the bluffs. The combined units were pinned down by Indian snipers. One company attempted to advance along the river bluffs and join Custer, but it was halted by a barrage of bullets from

Indian rifles. As darkness loomed, Reno and Benteen ordered their men to retreat to a more tenable position in the bluffs. Their soldiers were unable to join Custer's portion of the 7th Cavalry.

About the time that Reno had made his retreat, Custer and his 225 troops picked their way along the gully-cut ridge opposite the Indian camp and reached a point of descent leading to a place where the river could be crossed. As the troops neared the crossing, they were swarmed upon by Sioux, led by the warrior Gall. Two companies of troops dismounted for hand-to-hand combat, while Custer withdrew to a hilltop where he assumed a defensive position.

Some Indian sharpshooters zeroed in on horsemen. Others stampeded the cavalry pack horses that carried the vital ammunition supply for Custer's troops. At the same time Gall, now supported by warriors who had repulsed Reno, made a frontal attack from the south. The Northern Cheyenne under Brave Wolf and Lame White Man struck Custer's right flank and more Cheyenne attacked from the rear.

Custer was caught in a murderous crossfire as the warriors—superior in numbers and arms—made their charge. It probably did not take long—an hour or less—for the Sioux and Northern Cheyenne to overrun the embattled remnants of Custer's Seventh Cavalry. When General Terry finally arrived on June 27 to relieve Reno and Benteen, who were still pinned down, he found a terrible scene of carnage.

Old Wolf (standing) and Lame White Man—shown here in 1873—helped fight Custer at Little Bighorn.

The Indians, warriors and women alike, had swarmed over the battlefield, counting coups, stripping the dead troopers of their clothes and belongings, and shooting the near-dead and already dead. Custer, while stripped of his clothing, had not been scalped or mutilated, nor had most of his troops. The disaster of June 25, 1876, shocked the United States—not only the government but also ordinary citizens. To this day, "Custer's Last Stand" remains one of the most celebrated events of the

Old West, the topic of fiction, films, and ongoing debate: Was Custer betrayed by his own vanity or by the incompetence of his subordinates?

The Little Bighorn was also the last glorious stand of Cheyenne warriors. After defeating Custer, the Northern Cheyenne withdrew deep into the wild country, aware that the whites would seek to avenge this grave loss. They were right. A new Indian hunting expedition was organized almost imme-diately under General Ranald S. Mackenzie. His first objective was to capture Red Cloud's village of Sioux, which was assigned to the Pine Ridge Agency. He accomplished this quickly in 1876 and then left Ft. Fetterman and moved northward toward the Powder River in Wyoming. On November 26, Mackenzie's troops, supported by Paw-nee scouts plus Shoshone and Ban-nock, located and surrounded Dull Knife's village of Northern Cheyenne

The retreat of Major Marcus Reno's troops during the Battle of Little Bighorn. This drawing was made in the late 1800s by Oglala Sioux artist Amos Bad Heart Buffalo.

Cheyenne leaders Dull Knife (seated) and Little Wolf in the 1870s, when they sought to stay in their homeland. They found refuge with the Sioux.

on the Crazy Woman Fork of the Powder. In a dawn attack, they assaulted and destroyed the village, overcoming fierce resistance.

The survivors fled into the snow-bound hills and canyons. Many—including Dull Knife and Little Wolf—eventually found refuge with the Sioux. Despite that tribe's hospitality, the Cheyenne sank into destitution. They possessed few horses, robes, or blankets and had no food. They struggled through a terrible winter, and in April 1877, Dull Knife was forced to surrender at Ft. Robinson, Nebraska. Other Cheyenne also turned themselves over to U.S. authorities.

Now the government could accomplish by force what it had failed to do by treaty—remove the Cheyenne of the north and consolidate them with the Southern Cheyenne in the Oklahoma Indian Territory. When the northerners still refused to leave their beloved high country, their food rations were withheld. Finally they agreed to go, but only on a trial basis.

During the summer and early fall about 1,000 Northern Cheyenne began a grueling 70-day trek from Ft. Robinson, in the northern tip of Nebraska, to the Darlington Agency near El Reno, Oklahoma. They walked under a blazing sun, and nearly two-thirds of the group were stricken by an epidemic of fever and ague. The survivors vowed that someday they would make it back home. ▲

In the 20th century, most Cheyenne abandoned their lodges for more conventional homes. Here a Cheyenne builds modern housing on reservation grounds. By and large, the tribe has abandoned its traditional nomadism.

MODERN TIMES

Bad as reservation life in the Oklahoma Indian Territory was for the Southern Cheyenne, it proved much worse for the Northern Cheyenne. It cost them mightily to leave the high, dry country of the North, with its ample reserves of game, for the humid flatlands almost bereft of buffalo and deer. Hunger and sickness haunted them during the winter of 1877–78 and into the following summer. Despair sharpened Cheyenne resistance to the U.S. government's plans to turn them into farmers and to indoctrinate them into a new way of life.

As conditions worsened, the Northern Cheyenne chiefs plotted a return to their home ranges. "I am going north to my own country," Chief Little Wolf told Agent John D. Miles. "I do not want to see blood spilt about this agency. Let me get a little distance away from this agency. Then if you want to fight, I will fight you, and we can make the ground bloody at that place."

On the night of September 7, 1878, some 353 Northern Cheyennes left their campfires burning and tipi poles standing and began the trek north under Little Wolf, Dull Knife, and other chiefs. They had gone only a short distance when the alarm sounded behind them. Two troops of the 4th Cavalry, led by Captain Joseph Rendlebrock, hotly pursued them. Two days later the enemies fought at Turkey Springs, north of the Cimarron River. The Cheyenne warrior force—which included about 160 men and boys—held off the soldiers, killing 3 and wounding 3 more. Five Cheyennes were badly hurt.

The Cheyenne fled north into Kansas and again were intercepted, this time by Camp Supply troops who met them south of the Arkansas River. Little Wolf led a charge against the army supply wagons and captured some ammunition. The Cheyenne wanted to avoid a major struggle, however, and withdrew from the field at dark. They pressed northward, traveling through the night. On the Arkansas River, the

Cheyenne met and captured a group of buffalo hunters. Little Wolf ordered them released without harm and took only 18 slaughtered buffalo for his people to eat.

While still in Kansas, the Cheyenne met a third detachment of troops. The Cheyenne prevailed again, routing the enemy with close-range gunfire. The exodus continued into northwestern Kansas, where the Cheyenne came upon civilians along the Sappa and Beaver rivers. The Indians slew some white men for their horses but did not harm women or children.

Finally, the Northern Cheyenne entered the country beyond the Platte River, in Nebraska, and there divided into two groups. Little Wolf took one contingent to the Powder River country—in Wyoming and Montana—where they surrendered peacefully to U.S. troops. Later, Little Wolf and some of his men served as scouts for General Nelson A. Miles in his war against the Sioux. The second group of Cheyenne—about 150 strong—followed Dull Knife to the Red Cloud Agency near Ft. Robinson, Nebraska. They surrendered, yielded up their arms, and were held prisoner in a large, unheated building.

Soon conditions became unbearable. The Cheyenne went seven days without fire, food, or water, and many froze and starved. In desperation, they decided to face the soldiers' bullets or to brave the weather outdoors rather than perish helplessly inside the building. On January 9, 1879, Dull Knife's

people made a frantic charge for freedom. They leaped from the windows of their prison and dashed toward the surrounding hills. A few of the warriors had secretly hidden guns in the folds of the women's clothing. They now used them to fend off the soldiers while their women and children escaped.

The heroic attempt failed. Sixty-five of the 150 Cheyennes were recaptured, many of them wounded, and the frozen bodies of 50 more were found in the nearby hills by a detail of soldiers. Some Cheyenne disappeared altogether. The survivors were sent to the Pine Ridge Agency and assigned to their own agency in Montana. A few of the chiefs involved in the Northern Cheyenne's flight were later taken to Ft. Dodge, Kansas, to be tried for the murder of a white man. The charges were eventually dropped, and the chiefs returned to the Indian Territory and accepted the fate of reservation life.

While Dull Knife and his people were being held at Ft. Robinson, the U.S. government shifted another large group of Northern Cheyenne, led by Little Chief, south to the Indian Territory. Little Chief's band encountered the same oppressive conditions faced by their northern kin: sickness, scant food, cornmeal that made them sick, resentment by the Southern Cheyenne, and pressure from agents to adopt a way of life they detested.

Little Chief spoke for his people when he told the agent: "I was in good condition then [in the North]; now, look and see how poor I am growing

In 1879, Little Chief persuaded U.S. officials to let his people return to the Pine Ridge Reservation in South Dakota.

Indian agent John D. Miles led an expedition of Cheyenne chiefs to Washington, D.C., in the fall of 1873.

since I came down here. . . . We all would rather be among those mountains and streams where we were raised . . . we never get sick there. I was used to living by hunting all the time. It does not make me feel good to hang about an agency and have to beg a white man for something to eat when I get hungry."

Little Chief struggled to restrain his warriors during the next three years of hardship and difficulty, and in 1879 the Cheyenne leader took his case to Washington, D.C. He persuaded authorities to allow him and his people back on the Pine Ridge Agency, though they did not receive formal permission to return there until 1881.

During the 1880s, the Cheyenne still living in the Indian Territory fell victim to broken promises and self-contradictory government policies. Unable to hunt buffalo, which had been wiped off the Western plains by hordes of white hunters, the Indians grew increasingly dependent on the government. At the same time, they suffered continued mistreatment by whiskey dealers, unscrupulous traders, and white horse thieves.

Agent Miles initiated several programs meant to aid the Cheyenne.

Some met with more success than others. Efforts to make farmers of Cheyenne men did not work, and after several years the idea was abandoned. Miles had better luck with the Cheyenne-Arapaho Transportation Company. This project called for the hiring of Cheyenne and Arapaho as teamsters, or wagon drivers, who hauled their own goods and other freight from Kansas railheads to the agency. Miles purchased 40 wagons and harnesses, and soon Indian teamsters regularly drove the trail in Kansas between the Darlington Agency, Wichita, and Arkansas City.

Miles had another promising idea—establishing a cattle herd on the agency. He reasoned that it would feed the tribe and also train Cheyenne youths in stock tending and ranching. He was proved right on both counts as the herd grew in size and helped avert a food crisis. Then officials in Washington, D.C., leveled charges of corruption against the agency and ordered an end to Indian cattle raising. Miles then set up a policy whereby the Indians leased grasslands to outside cattlemen. Again he was foiled: Officials ordered him to rid the reservation of all cattle not owned by the Indians. Eventually Miles overcame this opposition, and the Cheyenne developed a sizable operation. However, troubles arose between the Indians and the cattlemen, and criticism of the program persisted until Miles was forced to resign in 1884.

His replacement, D. B. Dyer, reverted to the old policy of making farmers out of the Cheyenne. They resisted strongly, led by Stone Calf and Little Robe. The Dog Soldiers, only some of whom had disbanded, remained a serious hindrance to Dyer's efforts. They destroyed fences, killed cattle and horses, and threatened fellow Cheyenne with serious harm. Tensions mounted, and additional troops were brought into Ft. Reno, which sat just across the North Canadian River from Darlington.

In July 1885, generals Philip Sheridan and Nelson Miles arrived to investigate the problem. Sheridan let the Indians and cattlemen voice their complaints, but this attempt at fair-mindedness was undercut by President Grover Cleveland, who summarily ordered the reservation cleared of non-Indian cattle. A new agent, Captain Jesse M. Lee, replaced Dyer and removed some 210,000 head of cattle from Indian land. Cheyenne chiefs and the Dog Soldiers took solace in having thwarted the government.

But this victory was short-lived. The entire structure of Cheyenne society would soon be imperiled. The first blow came in 1887 with the passage of the Dawes, or General Allotment, Act. This federal legislation decreed that the president could allot reservation lands owned collectively by the tribe to individual tribe members, whom it reclassified as landowners and then as citizens subject to the laws of the state or territory where they lived. The act also provided for the sale of surplus reservation lands to whites.

The Dawes Act scattered the Southern Cheyenne on clusters of small farms along the North Canadian, South Canadian, and Washita rivers. This fragmented the tribe, unhinged its social structure, and blunted the influence of chiefs and war societies. Internal strife and factionalism now weakened the tribe. The Cheyenne forsook their own ceremonies and became caught up in the Ghost Dance religion devised in the late 1880s by the Paiute medicine man Wovoka. He and his priests claimed to have conversed with Christ, who granted them a vision that predicted the removal of whites from the Indian country within two years and a return to the old days of the buffalo hunts and

This drawing, made in 1878, details the layout of the Cheyenne-Arapaho Agency in north central Oklahoma.

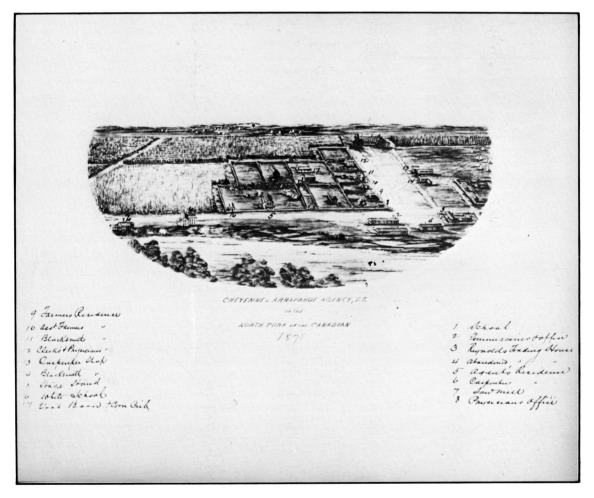

A Cheyenne council gathers for a Ghost Dance ceremony in the 1890s, when the religion was in vogue.

Indian supremacy. When the two years were up, however, neither prediction had come true, and the Ghost Dance fell out of favor among most tribes.

In 1889, on the heels of the Dawes Act, came another crushing blow: the opening up to white settlement of the Unassigned Lands, which lay in the heart of the Indian Territory and abutted the Cheyenne-Arapaho reservation (known, by this time, as the "Oklahoma Country"). A tumultuous land rush ensued. Then the government tried to purchase the surplus Cheyenne-Ara-

paho reservation lands from the tribes. Chief Old Crow spoke for his people when he told U.S. commissioners: "The Great Spirit gave the Indians all this country and never tell them that they should sell it. . . . I don't want money; money doesn't do an Indian any good."

But government pressure proved too much, and a sale agreement was eventually reached, though the Cheyenne challenged its validity, arguing that the document had not been signed by 75 percent of adult males, as required by law. Nonetheless, Congress approved the Cheyenne-Arapaho cession pact on March 3, 1891, and the era of the reservation came to an end for the southern tribes.

A year later, when the Cheyenne-Arapaho reservation was opened to white settlement, the amount of land still controlled by the tribes had been reduced from more than 4 million acres to 529,692. Much of what remained would be lost in the years ahead through a variety of tactics, including illegal taxation, crooked business dealings, and outright thievery. The Indians tried to protect themselves, but they stood no chance of gaining justice in the biased courts of the recently established Oklahoma Territory.

As if these setbacks were not enough, the entire culture of the Cheyenne came under attack in the 1890s when agent A. E. Woodson, a stern former military officer, campaigned to diminish the power of Cheyenne chiefs. He stripped their authority to issue rations within their tribe and thus humbled chiefs into standing in line with their followers for handouts. He out-

In 1889, settlers staked out lots in the newly created Oklahoma City, which would become the state capital when Oklahoma was admitted to the union 18 years later.

lawed sacred Cheyenne ceremonies, such as the Sun Dance and Medicine Arrow rites. He dispersed the Indians onto individual and isolated land allotments in order to break up their communal camp life. He also sought to stop gambling and the use of peyote, the drug introduced to Cheyenne culture along with the Ghost Dance. Finally, Woodson invoked territorial law to prohibit Cheyenne men from keeping more than one wife at a time.

Old Crow and other chiefs strenuously resisted this attack on their way of life, and most Southern Cheyenne clung to their accustomed ways. But the odds were stacked against them. It was easier to become a farmer or to seek out

This photograph, taken in 1901, shows Cheyenne slaughtering cattle. The tribe prospered at this trade until 1914, when the U.S. government outlawed communally owned herds.

the few jobs offered by white society than to practice dying customs. Some Cheyenne began to abandon their habitual style of dress, cut their long hair, move into wood-frame houses instead of tipis, and bow to the restraints and laws of the larger society that surrounded them.

Similar difficulties and upheavals beset the Northern Cheyenne. In 1884 they had been given a small reservation on the Tongue River in Montana, and in the years to come they subsisted on wild berries and fruits and killed the few animals that still roamed free. By century's end, the Northern Cheyenne resumed farming, raising corn and other vegetables as the Cheyenne had more than 100 years ago, before they became buffalo hunters.

As well as they could, they lived off the land. They cut hay from the rich grasslands of their reservation and sold it to nearby ranchers. They also sold firewood and worked as wagon drivers. And they continued to thrive as horse breeders. They expertly tended the few beasts they had taken with them to the reservation and produced fine herds that brought good prices from ranchers and the U.S. cavalry.

In the early 1900s, the government furnished individual tribesmen with small starting herds of cows and bulls, and the situation of the Northern Cheyenne improved. The men of the tribe soon proved themselves as capable with cattle as with horses, and the size of their herds steadily increased. But this new prosperity was halted in 1914,

when the Bureau of Indian Affairs decreed that the individually owned herds had to be consolidated into a single tribal herd. This dictate embittered Cheyenne cattle owners, who had to choose between relinquishing their herds or watching them be removed by soldiers. Thieves, hard winters, and wolves soon depleted the herd. It was hit particularly hard and greatly reduced during the bitterly cold winters of 1919 and 1920.

Bad times worsened in 1919 when the BIA decreed that a large number of Cheyenne horses would have to be destroyed in order to make more grassland available to the cattle herds. Many of the horses were shot, and their meat became rations for the tribe. Others were sold off—without a cent of the proceeds going to the Cheyenne. Their herd shrank from 15,000 head to 3,000, an incalculable loss to the horse-loving tribe.

Their horses disappeared, and so did their land. In the 1920s, the government tried to persuade the Northern Cheyenne to divide their reservation by allotting portions of land to individual tribesmen. Initially the Cheyenne staunchly opposed the arrangement, but eventually accepted it in 1933. Each member received 160 acres, and less than half the total land remained under tribal control.

In the late 19th and early 20th century, the Northern Cheyenne struggled to keep alive their ancestral culture. But the forces ranged against them were powerful. The most insistent call of

As early as the 1860s, the Darlington Agency was run by missionaries. First came Quakers, then Mennonites (shown here), who opened a school.

white authorities was that Cheyenne be sent to school, a concession the Dog Soldiers fought by pressuring their people to maintain their old ways. But by the 1880s, peace chiefs began to soften their opposition, and a few children appeared in classrooms. A mission school opened at Darlington in 1881, run by the Mennonite church, and an-

other school opened at the former army post at Cantonment, northwest of Darlington. Eventually, some Cheyenne boys went to Carlisle Institute in Pennsylvania and Hampton Institute in Virginia.

Only a small minority of Cheyenne children received schooling, however. In 1889 it was estimated that only one out of six Cheyenne knew the English language well enough to speak or understand it. And only about a quarter of those had much formal schooling. As for the rest, once they graduated, they remained outsiders, shut out of the American mainstream. Most went back home and resumed their lives within the tribe.

In subsequent decades the Southern and Northern Cheyenne suffered setbacks, but they came to contrasting fates. The Southern Cheyenne still live in poverty and continue to suffer the prejudice of their white neighbors. However, more opportunities are available to them than in previous times and a greater percentage of Southern Cheyenne now receive an education and pursue the material rewards long scorned by the tribe. As options opened up outside their reservation in south central Oklahoma, their population dropped—from 6,674 in 1970 to 5,220 in 1985.

The Northern Cheyenne have enjoyed much greater prosperity. In the late 1960s, vast quantities of coal were discovered beneath the soil of their reservation on the southeast tip of Montana. This mineral was greatly in demand, and the Northern Cheyenne saw history repeat itself as their land was overrun by new invaders, this time huge coal and energy corporations working in league with a long-time foe, the U.S. government. Yet again, the Cheyenne were ill-used by those supposed to aid them: On the advice of the BIA, they signed away the mineral

rights to more than half their reservation in return for large bonuses offered by the coal companies.

Soon they realized that the companies' plans for massive strip mines and power plants could mean the destruction of their habitat. They enlisted the help of George Crossland, a young BIA staff lawyer and an Osage. He advised them of illegal provisions in the contracts they had signed, and the Northern Cheyenne petitioned for the agreements to be cancelled. They did not regain everything they sought, but managed to protect their land and environment and to ensure themselves a secure future. At last, they scored a clear victory against their oppressors and exercised control over their own lives. For this reason, the population of the Northern Cheyenne reservation has recently climbed—from 2,100 in 1970 to 3,177 in 1985.

Today both branches of the Cheyenne nation inhabit a world defined partly by white society and partly by their own traditions. They drive automobiles, eat hamburgers, and enjoy popular music. But they also hold traditional powwows and cherish their ancestral celebrations, dances, songs, and games. Some Cheyenne rue the dimming of cherished tribal lore and blame the influence of white society. Others blame the tribe itself for giving in to the demands of the larger culture. In any case, the choice between the present and the past is not an easy one for a people who have become aliens in a land they once claimed as their own. ▲

BIBLIOGRAPHY

Ashabranner, Brent. *Morning Star, Black Sun*. Dodd, Mead & Company: New York, 1982.

Berthrong, Donald J. *The Cheyenne and Araphaho Ordeal*. Norman: University of Oklahoma Press, 1976.

————. *The Southern Cheyennes*. Norman: University of Oklahoma Press, 1963.

Bonner, T. D. *The Life and Adventures of James P. Beckwourth*. New York: Alfred A. Knopf, 1931.

Grinnell, George Bird. *The Fighting Cheyennes*. Norman: University of Oklahoma Press, 1956.

Hoebel, E. Adamson. *The Cheyennes: Indians of the Great Plains*. New York: Holt, Rinehart and Winston, 1960.

Hoig Stan. *The Battle of the Washita*. New York: Doubleday, 1976.

————. *The Peace Chiefs of the Cheyennes*. Norman: University of Oklahoma Press, 1980.

————. *The Sand Creek Massacre*. Norman: University of Oklahoma Press, 1961.

Hyde, George E., and Savoie Lottinville, eds. *Life of George Bent*. Norman: University of Oklahoma Press, 1967.

Llewellyn, Karl N., and E. Adamson Hoebel. *The Cheyenne Way*. Norman: University of Oklahoma Press, 1941.

Penoi, Charles. *No More Buffaloes*. Yukon, Oklahoma: Pueblo Publishing Press, 1981.

Powell, Peter J. *Sweet Medicine*. 2 vols. Norman: University of Oklahoma Press, 1969.

THE CHEYENNE AT A GLANCE

TRIBE *Cheyenne*

CULTURE AREA *Great Plains*

TRADITIONAL GEOGRAPHY *Northern Cheyenne—Wyoming and southern Montana—Southern Cheyenne—eastern Colorado and Kansas.*

LINGUISTIC FAMILY *Algonquian*

CURRENT POPULATION *Southern Cheyenne/Arapaho: 9,000; Northern Cheyenne: less than 4,000.*

FIRST CONTACT *René-Robert Cavelier, Sieur de La Salle, French, 1680*

FEDERAL STATUS *Recognized*

GLOSSARY

adobe A building material of straw and earth dried in the sun.

agent or **Indian agent** A person appointed by the Bureau of Indian Affairs to supervise U.S. government programs on a reservation and/or in a specific region; after 1908 the title "superintendent" replaced "agent."

Algonkian The Indian peoples living in the northeastern United States and east central Canada whose languages are related and who share numerous cultural characteristics.

allotment A U.S. policy applied nationwide through the General Allotment Act of 1887, intended to bring Indians into the mainstream by breaking up tribally owned reservations and tribal governments. Each tribal member was given, or allotted, a tract of land for farming.

Bow String Society or **Bow String Soldiers** One of five Cheyenne warrior societies. The others were called Fox, Elk, Shield, and Dog. Each society had distinctive styles of dress, dance, and song, as well as particular rituals and rules of behavior.

Bureau of Indian Affairs (BIA) A U.S. government agency established in 1824 and assigned to the Department of the Interior in 1849. Originally intended to manage trade and other relations with Indians and especially to supervise tribes on reservations, the BIA is now involved in programs that encourage Indians to manage their own affairs and improve their educational opportunities and general social and economic well-being.

calumet A long pipe ornamented with feathers and scalp locks, used in Cheyenne ceremonies.

clan A multigenerational group that has a common identity, organization, and property and that claims descent from a common ancestor. Because clan members consider themselves closely related, marriage within the clan is strictly prohibited.

counting coups The act of touching an enemy with a crook-ended stick during battle, a sign of great prowess.

Dog Soldiers The most powerful and feared of the five Cheyenne warrior societies.

Ghost Dance Religion or **Ghost** or **Spirit Dance** A religious movement that spread among Indians during the late 1880s centering on the belief that non-Indian newcomers would disappear and the Indians' traditional world would return if they enacted certain rituals, including dance movements performed for days at a time.

heum A special seat reserved for the Sweet Medicine Chief inside the council tipi. It signified his position as representative of the earth-governing deity.

Indian Territory An area in the south central United States where the U.S. government wanted to resettle Indians from other regions, especially the eastern states. In 1907 the territory became the state of Oklahoma.

kinnikinnick Tobacco, bark, dried leaves, herbs, and buffalo bone marrow blended together for smoking.

Massa'ne The comical antics of dancers dressed like animals in the Massaum Dance.

parfleche A folded, rectangular container made of rawhide, used for storing dried foods, blankets, and clothing.

peyote A cactus native to the southwestern United States and northern Mexico. The buttons of the cactus are sometimes eaten as part of Indian religious ceremonies.

Quakers The familiar name for members of the Religious Society of Friends, a mystical and pacifist group founded in England by George Fox in the 17th century. Quakers were active in efforts to help Indians during the 19th century.

Quiller's Society An exclusive women's group skilled in quill embroidery. The Quiller's Society supervised and instructed others in making quilled robes and observed certain rituals.

Renewal of Medicine Arrows An elaborate religious rite meant to renew the four Sacred Arrows and to unify the tribe.

Sun Dance A religious rite highlighted by ceremonial dancing, it symbolized renewal of the world and often included self-torture.

tipi A conical dwelling of the Plains tribes that consisted of a circular framework of poles joined at the top and covered with animal hides.

treaty A contract negotiated between representatives of the United States and one or more Indian tribes. Treaties dealt with surrender of political independence, peaceful relations, land sales, boundaries, and related matters.

tribe A type of society consisting of a community or group of communities that occupy a common territory and are related by bonds of kinship, language, and shared traditions.

INDEX

PICTURE CREDITS

STAN HOIG is professor emeritus at Central State University, Edmond, Oklahoma, where he taught journalism for more than 20 years. His books include *The Humor of the American Cowboy*, *The Sand Creek Massacre*, *The Western Odyssey of John Simpson Smith*, *The Battle of the Washita*, *The Peace Chiefs of the Cheyennes*, *David L. Payne: The Oklahoma Boomer*, and *The Oklahoma Land Rush of 1889*. He has also published many articles in popular and professional magazines, and in 1976 he wrote the book and music for a historical pageant entitled "Oklahoma, U.S.A." Hoig holds a B.A. from Oklahoma State University and an M.A. and Ph.D. from the University of Oklahoma.

FRANK W. PORTER III, General Editor of INDIANS OF NORTH AMERICA, is Director of the Chelsea House Foundation for American Indian Studies. He holds a M.A, B.A., and Ph.D. from the University of Maryland. He has done extensive research concerning the Indians of Maryland and Delaware and is the author of numerous articles on their history, archaeology, geography, and ethnography. He was formerly Director of the Maryland Commission on Indian Affairs and American Indian Research and Resource Institute, Gettysburg, Pennsylvania, and he has received grants from the Delaware Humanities Forum, the Maryland Committee for the Humanities, the Ford Foundation, and the National Endowment for the Humanities, among others. Dr. Porter is the author of *The Bureau of Indian Affairs* in the Chelsea House KNOW YOUR GOVERNMENT series.